SOUL WILDERNESS

For Chan,
who knew the desert

You shall love the nothing,
You shall flee from the something,
You shall stand alone,
And go to no one.
You shall not be very industrious
And be free from all things;
You shall free the captives
And restrain the free;
You shall refresh the sick
And still take nothing for yourself;
You shall drink the water of pain
And kindle the fire of love with the wood of
virtue.
Then will you live in the true desert.

Mechtild of Magdeburg

KERRY WALTERS

Soul Wilderness

A Desert Spirituality

● PAULIST PRESS ● New York/Mahwah, N.J.

Biblical texts are cited according to the Revised Standard Version (RSV) of the bible. The Publisher gratefully acknowledges use of the following: Excerpt from "Jeronimo's House" from *The Complete Poems* by Elizabeth Bishop. Copyright 1999. Reprinted by permission of Farrar, Straus and Giroux. Excerpt from "Great flaming God, bend to my troubles dear" from *Henry's Fate and Other Poems* by John Berryman. Copyright 1977. Reprinted by permission of Farrar, Straus and Giroux. Excerpt from "The Night Journey" from *Works* by Rupert Brooke. Copyright 1994. Reprinted by permission of Wordsworth Editions, Ltd. Excerpt from "The Hanging Man" from *Collected Poems* by Sylvia Plath. Copyright 1965 by Ted Hughes. Reprinted by permission of Faber and Faber, Ltd., and Harper-Collins Publishers, Inc. Excerpts from "Four Quartets" from *Collected Poems 1909–1962* by T. S. Eliot. Reprinted by permission of Faber and Faber, Ltd.

Publisher's acknowledgments continue on page 155

TYPE DESIGN • CASA PETTA

COVER DESIGN • CYNTHIA DUNNE

Library of Congress Cataloging-in-Publication Data

Walters, Kerry S.
    Soul wilderness : a desert spirituality / Kerry Walters.
        p. cm.
    Includes bibiographical references.
    ISBN 0-8091-4007-1
    1. Spirituality—Catholic Church. 2. Deserts—Religious aspects—Christianity. 3. Wilderness (Theology) 1. Title.
    BX2350.2 .W35 2000
    248.4′82—dc21

                                                    00-046495

Published by Paulist Press
997 Macarthur Boulevard
Mahwah, New Jersey 07430

www.paulistpress.com

Printed and bound in the
United States of America

Contents

Contents

Acknowledgments

Of all my books, this has been the hardest to get down on paper—partly because poetry is the *lingua terra* of soul wilderness, and I, alas, am no poet; partly because much of the book was written during a time when I myself was flayed by the desert sirocco.

Thanks to those kind persons who endured, especially Kim, Jonah, Lisa, and Karmen; to Professor Ilse Bulhof, who nudged me toward a better understanding of divine nothingness; and to Kathleen Walsh, editor good and true, who patiently awaited the manuscript.

The book is offered in memory of my friend Chan Coulter, whose passing still tears my heart.

Chapter One

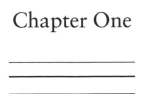

Desert Revelations

They cannot scare me with their empty spaces
Between stars—on stars where no human race is.
I have it in me so much nearer home
To scare myself with my own desert places.
                                    Robert Frost
I would like to step out of my heart
and go walking beneath the enormous sky.
                                    Rainer Maria Rilke

Ambiguous Landscape

To find God, we must go to the desert. Once there, we discover that the desert, like God, is a great mystery. It's never quite what it appears to be, and our responses to it are never simple.

Sometimes the desert reveals itself as barren wasteland, a wilderness of desolate exile. The sun is merciless, the soil sterile, the terrain alternately hostile or monotonous. Those few creatures hardy enough to thrive in the desert are stamped by their blighted environment: the viper, the sullen lizard, the scorpion—grotesque imps from a Bosch painting. Even the scant and dusty brush is inhospitable, its thorns belligerent warnings to trespassers. Death dwells here, we murmur to ourselves. "This is dead land/This is cactus land...."[1] Our minds fill with visions of bleached bones amid red rock and silent sand, and we recoil in horror. We say: The desert is no place for people like us.

But sometimes the desert reveals another face. The desolation that once crushed us now whispers of clean transparency and pregnant silence, a "fusion," as one wilderness sojourner put it, "of pure elements from the heavens above and the earth beneath...untrammeled and untouched by anything [humanly] contrived."[2] The stark emptiness of the desert no longer oppresses. Now it seems our natural element, the one place we can finally open our eyes and stretch our limbs. We quit our tents and breathe the clear air and gaze at the horizon and say: I could dwell in such a place. I could put down roots here. This could be my home.

The desert, the wilderness, both repulses us and beckons to us. Sometimes we see it as horror, sometimes as haven. This ambivalence isn't a sign of confusion on our part. The desert is a paradox, and all paradoxes call forth complicated responses.

The desert paradox is deeply rooted. In a God-ordered universe, the outer world is a *figura,* an emblem, of the inner one. When we thrill to beauty or shudder at blemish in the physical world, we do so because these sensible phenomena conjure memories of their spiritual counterparts within our souls and send shock waves of recognition pulsing through us. Like calls to like: The outer world croons its ambiguous song and we hear echoing melodies from the interior one. Our responses to the physical desert, then, are born from the chthonic awareness that its sensible landscape is the cipher of a spiritual one. Our eyes gaze upon physical terrain, but our hearts intuit soul wilderness.

This interior desert, like its external counterpart, is a frightening and wondrous place. It's frightening because demons, every bit as menacing as the viper or grotesque as the scorpion, crouch beneath its dry red rocks, eager to waylay us. These demons are the shadow sides of the self, monstrosities we normally keep deeply buried so that we need not consciously confront them. But the inner landscape isn't just a barren and dangerous wasteland. It's also a place of holy emptiness and solitude and purification and promise. The palpable presence of God is there, the divine white noise of beating wings, the haunting chord of silent music.

Soul wilderness is the place where God dwells. It's from the inner desert that God speaks to our hearts. If we would hear the divine voice, we must abide in the desert until we break through to its secret. This means embracing a desert spirituality which takes us deep into the silence and solitude of our interior landscape.

Desert Koan

A paradox (*para*=beyond; *dokein*=to think) properly elicits from us a lived response, not a conceptual analysis. When we venture into the inner desert, we enter a mysterious realm that stubbornly resists the battering ram of reason. Soul wilderness is a through-the-looking-glass place of incompatibilities and impossibilities, of longing that is also dread and complete emptiness that is also absolute fullness. When we go there, we dive inside the self to discover that which is radically not-self and yet supremely real-self. The trek across the sands of the heart leaves us blind but visionary, deaf but acutely sensitive, utterly destitute yet unimaginably replenished.

As if all this weren't baffling enough, here's another facet of the desert paradox: Soul wilderness is both the route and the destination. We don't venture into soul wilderness to work our way through to its other side. There is no other side, no promised land beyond the dunes. The desert of exile *is* the promised homeland. Divine milk and honey drip there or nowhere. Catherine of Siena famously said that all the way to heaven is heaven. She might just as well have said that all the way to desert is desert. God is *in* the desert. God *is* the desert. It is that divine place, Thomas Merton tells us, "whose center is everywhere and whose circumference is nowhere," and we traverse it only by "standing still."[3]

How can we make sense of this? The short answer is that we can't. The inner desert is a koan, akin to those spiritual riddles from the Rinsai Zen tradition whose pregnant paradoxicality births not conceptual comprehension but heart wisdom.

The working assumption behind a koan is simple enough: If a person is ever to achieve enlightenment, she must first clear her mind and soul of all intellectual preconceptions about the nature of things. These contrivances stand between her and a naked encounter with what is. Her problem is that she knows how to think, but not how to experience. To move from one to the other, she must let go of the conceptual filters through which she habitually strains reality.

So the Zen master gives the disciple a koan to chew on, a riddle that the intellect can't possibly unravel: "What's the sound of one hand clapping?" or "What did your face look like before you were born?" The hope is that weeks or months or years of meditation on the koan will so undermine the arrogant citadel of reason that it finally cracks and falls, thereby creating a vacuum into which reality rushes. When this happens, the disciple comes into immediate contact with what *is*. She experiences rather than merely thinks. She attains enlightenment.

A koan, then, has no solution. Instead, its purpose is to evoke an experience of the unutterable depth of existence, a truth-radiant moment intellectually unfathomable but so palpably meaningful for whoever encounters it that he or she enters into and becomes the koan. As William Butler Yeats once wrote, we can embody truth even if we can never know it.[4]

The Christian tradition is crammed with koans—in fact, it's not beyond the pale to say that Christianity *is* a koan.[5] How, after all, to make sense of the intellectual absurdity—God become human—that lies at its core? What could it possibly mean to say that the infinite becomes finite yet remains infinite, that the eternal takes on temporality without losing its eternality? From a rational perspective, it means precisely nothing. We can theologize about the hypostatic union of God and flesh in the person of Jesus until our heads spin, but we'll never understand what's going on in the incarnation because it's a koan that defies the intellect. The incarnation simply *is*, and in its is-ing reveals a great but incomprehensible truth about existence. We can experience this truth. We can live it. But it will always remain a paradox, a koan, which we'll never nail down with the hammer of reason. *Credo quia absurdum est.*

The incarnational koan that pulsates at the heart of Christianity spins off any number of familiar ancillary ones: *Whoever loves life will lose it. In order to live one must die. This is my body but also not my body, my blood but also not my blood. Loving means hating mother, father, wife, husband, child. Poverty is wealth.* To the ear of the intellect, all this is rubbish. But to the ear of a heart attuned to the primary desert experience rather than second-order rational abstractions, such koans ring with the vitality and solidity of reality. They are supremely meaningful, even if utterly absurd.

Soul wilderness is a revelatory koan we must enter into, experience, and live. As with all koans, the absurdity of the interior desert baffles and bewilders the mind. This is why it elicits such ambivalent responses from us. Soul wilderness *is* red rock and wings, desolation and presence, poverty and wealth, loneliness and encounter, death and life, self and not-self, the way and the goal, the unkingdom and the kingdom, not-God and God. Make no mistake about it: When we hazard the inner desert we both lose our way and find our way. As Meister Eckhart cryptically promised, in soul wilderness we find truth by discarding truth. In soul wilderness, we live in the Divine by living without the divine.[6]

There is no answer to the desert koan. That's one revelation. Here's another: The desert koan is its own answer.

Desert Adventure

To sink deeply into the koan of soul wilderness is to embark on the greatest human adventure. We tend to think of adventure as an Indiana Jones kind of undertaking that tests our strength and cunning. The valiant hero battling against risky and exciting dangers—this is what typically springs to mind.

It's true that adventures are dangerous times of testing. But it's also important to remember, especially when reflecting on what it means to journey into soul wilderness, that an adventure is essentially a quest for fulfillment, for completion. The word "adventure," after all, is derived from the Latin *advenire,* "to arrive." When we venture forth, we set out on a path that ultimately leads us where we need to go in order to become what we're meant to be. Once we get there we've "arrived," in the sense that we've embraced our destiny. This is the true—the spiritual—meaning of adventure, and it's echoed, howsoever dimly, in tales and legends of heroes from all times and cultures.

Whether the adventuring hero is an ugly duckling who becomes a swan, a bumbling apprentice learning the ways of magic, or a milkmaid who exchanges her rags for a queenly tiara, the pattern is the same: a journey whose very dangers and trials unveil one's true identity.

Those who cross the frontier into soul wilderness are heroes who embark on the greatest of all adventures because they search for the greatest of all destinies: God. Since its earliest days, Christianity has described itself as *hodos,* "the way," the path or road by which adventurous wayfarers journey to the Divine. The ancient Hebrews, Christianity's spiritual ancestors, established this precedent centuries before Christ. The very word "Hebrew" in fact appears to be derived from *habiru,* a Canaanite word for "traveler" or "pilgrim." Abraham and his children, Moses and the refugees from Egypt—all were *habiru,* wanderers seeking God's face in the great koan of the desert.

St. Paul recognized and accepted this wayfaring legacy when he reminded the Christians of Corinth that their Hebraic forefathers and mothers stumbled through the wilderness under a cloud of paradox (1 Cor 10:1). Since Paul's time, any number of saints and theologians have been equally struck by the desert journey as a metaphor for the Christian adventure. As Origen said in the third century, every Christian must strike out for the wilderness if he or she hopes to reach fulfillment. "The whole journey takes place," he wrote, "the whole course is run, for the purpose of arriving at the river of God, so that we may be made neighbors of the flowing wisdom and may be watered by the waves of divine knowledge."[7]

Journeys can be divided into stages. Joseph Campbell, the twentieth-century troubadour of spiritual adventure, claims there are no fewer than four in the wayfaring hero's journey toward completion in God.[8] Campbell's itinerary is especially illuminating for those who venture forth into soul wilderness. It doesn't demystify the koan of the desert; as koan, the desert forever remains paradoxical. But Campbell's stages do give us some idea of what we can expect to run across when we travel in and toward that unspeakable mystery that lies at the core of who we really are.

All of us carry soul wilderness within our hearts, and all of us occasionally catch fleeting glimpses of its terrain. But we tend to be so immersed in the busy everyday world that we pay little or no attention to these intuitions of an undiscovered country. Sometimes, however, the allure of the vaguely sensed inner desert overwhelms us, calling us from our immersion in the external world and driving us into the depths of the interior one. When this happens, we forsake our comfortable home and set out with fear and trembling into the unknown desert. This is the journey's first stage: We heed the call of the desert and leave home to follow it.

But almost immediately we encounter the red rock demons. How could we not? When we cross over into soul wilderness we dive deeply into the self, and the self is haunted by impish passions, howling thoughts, and wailing banshees of memory. Gerard Manley Hopkins only scratched the surface of soul wilderness in his terrifying evocation of it:

> O the mind has mountains; cliffs of fall
> Frightful, sheer, no-man-fathomed. Hold them cheap
> May who ne'er hung there.[9]

If we hope to advance any further into the desert, we must do battle with the imps who crouch in the mountains of the mind. Just as Christ descended into hell, so must we descend into our own inner inferno. The struggle there is the second stage in the journey toward completion. For many of us, it lasts an entire lifetime. The red rock demons are numberless as the desert sand.

Now the utter paradoxicality of the desert koan especially reveals itself. For the struggle with the demons who haunt the soul is always fatal. If we succumb to them, we lose the hope of finding our true self in the desert—and what is this but a living death? But if we rout and slay the demons, these noisy passions and terrors and lusts and habits that together make up the everyday self, then the everyday self necessarily dies as well. Burning down a vermin-infested house eradicates the vermin, but it also destroys the house. Either way, death awaits the desert traveler, and it is both dreadful and unavoidable.

Counterintuitive as it seems, however, the death we suffer in our defeat of the inner desert's demons is a necessary prelude to genuine life. For when the din of battle is over and the scouring wind—*ruach, pneuma,* spirit—bleaches and scatters our bones, what remains is the silent music, the pregnant emptiness, of the wilderness. This is the place where God dwells. The desert air grows pellucid and fragrant with the presence of the great nothingness which is God, and in that pure and untrammeled element, our true home, we are resurrected. We arrive at our destiny, our identity, our ultimate fulfillment. A wondrous fusion between the place of encounter, the divine object of encounter, and the encountering pilgrim occurs. As St. Paul said, it is not now the old self of red rock demons that lives, but rather the real self, the true self, the God-saturated self. The desert koan becomes completely meaningful for the resurrected and transformed self, even though it remains utterly mysterious. It is lived, not thought; experienced, not uttered. Miraculous rebirth from painful death—this is the third stage of the journey.

But this grand fusion that transfigures the desert, reveals God, and resurrects the true self isn't the final stage in the hero's journey. There's one more: the return. The person who has arrived at her destiny may long to remain forever in the desert of whirling wings and divine silence. But she realizes that the wilderness transformation has named her a prophet, an emissary of God. She now bears the fiery mark of the Divine and this summons her to collaborate in the divine task of guiding other souls into the wilderness. So she turns back to the everyday world of noisy distraction, the realm of false selves and leering demons, to share with others what she's discovered in the desert. This great secret, which she can only haltingly speak, is her boon to the world. She doesn't return with definitive answers, mind you, but rather with something much more precious: She returns as a living embodiment of the desert koan. It is her gift—it is *God's* gift—to humanity.

Desert Butterfly, Desert Rose

The desert koan and the spiritual pilgrim's journey into it are symbols of the mystical search for God. The mystic yearns for an immediate encounter with the Divine, for an unfiltered experience of the replete nothingness of God. Words, language, theory, are paltry things when it comes to God. They offer us abstractions or similes, which at best gesture toward the divine paradox and at worst become substitutes for it. Even the evocative language of poetry, the least artificial way to try to speak the koan, risks blocking our entry into the mystery. But the desert is a place of primordial silence, and silence makes room for encounter. So to the desert we must go if we would sink into the silence of God.

Another desert koan—to escape the relative nothingness of a life empty of God we must embrace the absolute nothingness of God.

That feisty woman of God, Teresa d'Avila, knew about the desert. She staggered across its salt flats and smelled fear in its red dust, but she also caught the silent music of its wings. She knew that the journey into the soul—into the many-roomed "interior castle," as she so wonderfully imagined it—was a mystical one of leave-taking (heeding the divine call), death (the purgative way), rebirth and transfiguration (infused union, the "spiritual marriage" between God and the soul), and return (abiding in and sharing divine love). One of St. Teresa's most striking metaphors for this mystical adventure is particularly appropriate in a discussion of soul wilderness. I'm referring to her famous description of the soul as a silkworm.

The silkworm is a wondrous creature, Teresa tells us, because it's a living parable of the scriptural koan (Col 3:3) that our true life is in God. Goaded by an inarticulate urge to become what it's intended to be, the silkworm withdraws from the world, plunges deeply into itself and, from the stuff found there, enshrouds itself in a tightly woven cocoon. The worm forsakes the everyday world of mulberry leaves and daylight to vanish into interior darkness. When the cocoon-tomb finally breaks open, what emerges is a beautiful white-winged butterfly. The earthbound worm is dead, transformed by its experience of utter darkness into a splendid creature of sky and sun.

A human is like a silkworm, and if we hope to grow into what we're intended to be, we must dive deeply into our own inner world and bury ourselves there. Soul wilderness is our cocoon, and our growing awareness of both its red rock dread and its winged promise is the inner stuff from which we spin our future. As we burrow more and more deeply into this desert, we too die: to the ego and to the world on the other side of the cocoon. But this is as it should be, Teresa reassures us. "Let the silkworm die—let it die, as in fact it does when it has completed the work which it was created to do. Then we shall see God and shall ourselves be as completely hidden in His greatness as is this little worm in its cocoon."[10] And when we enter into that great nothingness and are ourselves made greatly nothing through union with it, the desert becomes a place of transfiguration and rebirth.

No one wants to die, but all of us yearn in our hearts to become creatures of the air. We sense that the only way to do this is to undertake the perilous mystical journey into soul wilderness, to forsake the home to which we've grown accustomed for the uncharted desert whose mystery both terrifies and tantalizes. During one of the bleakest periods of his life, Merton came to appreciate the importance of undertaking this journey.

> I need something beyond my capacity to know....Silence, a primitive life. What I need—as far as I can interpret the desire to my heart—is to make a journey to a primitive place, among primitive people, and there die. It is at the same time a going out and a "return." A going to somewhere where I have never been or thought of going—a going in which I am led by God, a journey in which I go out from everything I have now. And I feel that unless I do this my spiritual life is at an end.[11]

When we wrap ourselves inside the cocoon-koan of soul wilderness, the "primitive," unadorned, and unknowable darkness of God, we journey to that distant country Merton pined for. We arrive where we are destined to be, and in that sense our going out is also a return. The silkworm dies and the butterfly emerges. "Oh, greatness of God," exclaims Teresa, "that a soul should come out like this after being hidden in the greatness of God and closely united with Him!"[12]

Some fifteen hundred years before Teresa, the anonymous author of the Psalms of Solomon, reflecting on his own sojourn in the wilderness, wrote these words:

> My heart was cloven and there appeared a flower
> and grace sprang up
> and fruit from the Lord.[13]

The desert will split open one's cocoon-heart, and from this dreadful and wonderful fracture a desert rose will blossom.

A Lamp Alight and Shining

The Hebrew and Christian scriptures are chronicles of the soul's struggle to enter into and live the desert koan. Predictably, biblical accounts of the wilderness are paradoxical.[14]

On the one hand, desert or wilderness (Hebrew=*midbar;* Greek=*eremos topos*) is a place of desolation, disorder, and danger. It is that which is beyond human settlements *(midbar),* that which is solitary or "desert-ed" *(eremos).* When one is in the wilderness, one is literally be-*wild*-ered: lost or disoriented in a threatening wasteland. Even slavery is seen as a desirable alternative to the desert (Exod 16:3), that "vast and dreadful wilderness" with "fiery serpents" and "scorpions" lurking amidst "hardest rock" (Deut 8:15). Wilderness is the place where both savage beasts (Ezek 34:25) and evil spirits (Luke 11:24) dwell, and the pilgrim who journeys there risks all.

On the other hand, wilderness is also described in Hebrew and Christian scripture as a place of solitary and silent encounter with the Divine. God can be found in the desert: In this sense, *midbar* indeed is the place beyond the world of distractions that induce forgetfulness of the Divine. Isaiah seeks the promised garden in the midst of the wasteland (the butterfly hidden in the cocoon, as it were), confident that living water flows underneath dry sand (43:20), and Hosea assures us that the desert is where God woos humans (2:14). Moreover, the desert harshness that so frightens and repels us sandblasts the tarnished soul until it's capable of reflecting God's darkly brilliant self-revelation. Abram receives the covenant in the desert (Gen 17), Moses and the children of Israel discover the great and mysterious "I AM" in their wilderness sojourn (Exod 3:14), and Elijah harkens to the divine refrain in the desert's resounding silence (1 Kgs 19:12).

All of these spiritual adventurers are exemplars of the desert traveler. They leave home, be it Ur or pharaoh's fleshpots, enter into the wilderness, are tested by the demons they encounter there, ultimately dive into and drown in the great desert emptiness of God, and come up again as newly born prophets ready to lead others into the wilderness.

In the Christian tradition, the greatest of all desert pilgrims is that elusive ascetic John the Baptist. No figure chronicled in Christian scripture was esteemed more by Jesus, who called John a "pattern of righteousness" (Matt 21:23), the culmination of the great prophetic tradition (Matt 11:13), and a "lamp alight and shining" with the spirit of God (Matt 11:11; Luke 7:28; John 5:35). John's heroic journey into the desert koan is archetypal. He is the guiding inspiration for all subsequent adventurers into soul wilderness.

We know that John was born in the fertile hill country of Judah to Elizabeth and Zechariah, both descendants of Aaron. We also know that there was something wondrous about his conception, heralded as it was by an angel of the

Lord who predicted a great destiny for the unborn child. John, like all the prophets before him, was called from the womb, given a face before he was born. His destiny, the angel proclaimed, was to be "filled with the Holy Spirit, and [to] bring back many of the sons [and daughters] of Israel to the Lord their God" (Luke 1:15–16).

A flashy start, this. But then silence. Scripture tells us almost nothing about the years between John's birth and his emergence as a prophet some thirty years later. The only hint is a laconic verse from Luke (1:80): "[T]he child grew up and his spirit matured. And he lived out in the wilderness until the day he appeared openly to Israel."

It's entirely in keeping with the koanic nature of soul wilderness for scripture to remain silent about John's time of testing. But we can infer this much: When John heeded the call of God and forsook a comfortable home for the uncertainty of the desert, he plunged into a spiritual crucible whose intense heat burned away the old John and birthed the Baptist. John ben Zechariah battled his demons in the desert and in slaying them died. From the ashes arose a man burning with the Divine—a man, Luke tells us, aglow with the silent but fiery word of God (3:2).

John's very appearance when he returned to the world attests to his desert transfiguration. The nattily attired and groomed priest's kid had vanished. In his place was a wild-haired, blazing-eyed apparition who scarcely bothered to cover his nakedness with a coarse camel's hair robe. His speech was just as rough and threatening as his appearance: not for the Baptist the dignified and safe tones of the pulpit. Those who saw him—including family and acquaintances who remembered the proper little yeshiva boy of bygone years—shook their heads in bewilderment. He's gone bonkers, they muttered. He's possessed (Matt 11:18; Luke 7:33).[15]

They were right, of course. John *was* possessed—by God. His sojourn in the wilderness liberated him from self and brought him that immediate and unsayable experience of God that is the true destiny of the spiritual pilgrim. Conventional piety gave way to the mystical and prophetic ardor that always strikes the world as madness. When one encounters the divine koan and is absorbed into its holy paradoxicality, when one surrenders to the sheer nothingness of God, decreasing so that the divine nothingness may increase, one necessarily becomes a holy fool.

And what foolishness this holy fool shouted! He stared into the eyes of perfectly respectable men and women, folks who observed the Law and considered themselves righteous children of God, and thundered at them to drop their pretensions and follow him into the desert. *Brood of vipers!* he cried. *You think the covenant is a substitute for venturing forth into soul wilderness? Leave home, perish in the silent emptiness of red rock and sand, and come back as emissaries of divine love. Cease fleeing from God the koan. Give up the security of conventional piety and plunge into the ocean of luminous paradox! Don't just think about God—experience God! Don't just read what Moses and the prophets wrote about God—discover it for yourselves! Don't struggle merely to live "properly"—live Godly! Repent: Turn away from home and back toward God, your true origin and final destination!*

The good and terrible news John the Baptist brought to his contemporaries, and to us as well, is that salvation is found in soul wilderness. Luke records (3:1–15) that their response (just like ours today) was predictably ambivalent: scandalized and frightened on the one hand—*what? leave our homes to perish amid the red rocks?*—and a curious sense of expectancy, of anxious nostalgia, on the other. John's auditors discovered the paradox that each succeeding generation has rediscovered: The desert is the place we most dread, and it's also the place for which our hearts primordially ache.

Desert Spirituality

John's message is unequivocal, even if the intellect can't fully grasp its depth. God dwells in the desert—God *is* the desert—and if we would find God we must go there. Nothing short of immediate contact with the divine fire will do, and this fire only burns in the wilderness. To be a Christian in the fullest sense—to arrive at one's destiny, to discover one's original face—it is necessary to brave the desert koan.

This means forsaking a spirituality that is safe but tepid. Karl Rahner wrote that "the devout Christian of the future will either be a 'mystic,' one who has experienced 'something,' or he [or she] will cease to be anything at all."[16] Theological speculation has its place, but a lived and living experience of God must be the primary focus. God, like the soul wilderness where God dwells, is a koan, ultimately hidden from the intellect behind an impenetrable cloud of unknowing. God is a God of silence, beyond what even the holiest discourse can communicate. At the end of the day, this God can be encountered but neither analyzed nor uttered. The mystic realizes this and, along with John, risks the desert adventure for the sake of the burning bush.

The silent presence of God is in the heart of each of us. Created as we are in the divine image, carrying in our soul the supreme artist's signature, we have, says Rahner, "an immediate, preconceptual experience of God through the experience of the limitless breadth of our consciousness."[17] The trick is to cultivate a spirituality which helps us make unfiltered contact with that experience. Conventional piety, lukewarm spirituality—what C. S. Lewis was fond of calling "whiskey-and-soda" (that is, watered down) Christianity—as well as abstract speculations and streams of words about God—all of these can numb us to the unsayable but totally real mystery of the indwelling God. When we go to the desert, we shed these soporifics one by one—or, more accurately, the desert strips them from us, liberating us to discover what the Baptist discovered. We enter into the mystic's way of purgative humility, reverent silence, and empty receptivity. We open ourselves to a God-experience that reveals our destiny and in so doing transforms us into who we really are.

But a mystic, as John's example shows us, is also a prophet. The person who undertakes the mystical journey into soul wilderness returns to the world aflame with the transfigurative encounter with God. The prophetic mandate is clear: to live and preach in such a way that emboldens others to leave the comforts of home in order to die the death of spiritual rebirth. This return demands just as much courage as the initial foray into the desert, because it means stirring up the waters, waging battle against spiritual sloth, risking the fury of the crowd. Courage is also demanded because of the ever present danger of prophetic zeal perverting into arrogant self-assertion. The red rock demons crouched in the mountains of the mind are tenacious, and living in the desert means one must always be on guard against them.

So once again the koan surfaces. The desert is a place at one and the same time frightening and appealing. God is a koan, unknowable yet supremely experiential, an empty presence, silent music. Embracing God in the desert is a koan: We die in order to be reborn. And living spiritually is a koan: sinking deeply into that deep core where God dwells and one's true identity is found, while at the same time throwing oneself whole-heartedly into the hurly-burly of the world as a crier of desert secrets.

A seemingly impossible task, this. A heroic task. But one to which all of us, without exception, are called.

An Atlas of Sorts

The pages that follow explore the "impossible" journey into soul wilderness you and I are called to undertake. But at the end of the day a book is just a book, and the telling of a story is no substitute for the living of it. As the poet Edmond Jabès points out, "a book [is] but a bit of fine sand taken from the desert one day and returned a few steps farther on."[18] So I make no greater claim here than to provide a rough atlas of the desert's terrain, and no one, of course, should confuse idling over a map with actually setting out on the journey. The thing is to go into the desert, to allow oneself to be absorbed by the divine koan, not merely to dream about doing so.

At the same time, however, an atlas can be of some aid in getting us started because it provides an overview of the geography that must be traversed in working toward our spiritual destination/destiny. Joseph Campbell has already provided us with some idea of the stages that define the soul's trek toward God. Campbell's typology, along with whatever directions we can pick up along the way from fellow-traveling poets, novelists, theologians, and philosophers, will help us plot the course of our own journey.

The first step in the exodus toward God is getting clear about the place we're already at, the place the heroic tradition calls "home." Whatever else the word "home" connotes, from a spiritual perspective it first and foremost suggests a comfortably familiar haven which protects us from the desert's frightening uncanniness. For the conventionally religious person, "home" is a pseudo-spirituality that centers around gods tailor-made to fit her own neurotic needs and egoistic desires. These gods and their accompanying spiritualities wear any number of faces, but each is characterized by the fact that it functions as a buffer against the life-threatening sand and wind of soul wilderness. Chapter 2 explores the most common of the "household gods" we timidly cling to in our efforts to avoid the desert.

But as Karl Rahner has already reminded us, each person is haunted by the presence of holiness. The true God, the God of the desert, blazes at the heart of soul wilderness, and the sirocco it churns up inevitably rips away our flimsy burnooses. Cling as we may to our household gods, the desert ceaselessly calls us to leave home and venture into its merciless waste. Sometimes the call is softly muted and gently alluring. But usually it comes during times of crisis and despair—what Rahner calls "decisive moments"—which sickeningly reveal to us the hollowness of our false gods and the sham play pretensions of our spirituality. The divine wind demolishes our homes, blows us to the desert's brink, and catapults us over the edge into the terrible koanic wasteland. This fall, the initial stage of the spiritual journey, is explored in chapter 3.

Chapter 4 examines the epic battle the pilgrim fights with the desert demons once she plunges into soul wilderness. The merciless light of the desert sun allows for no self-deception or dissimulation on our parts. It illuminates the most shadowy regions of the inner terrain, exposing the legion of imps lurking there. Spawned by the vain willfulness of their chief, the false or "pretender" self, these imps—passions, fears, lusts— furiously strive to turn us back to human habitation, back to the opium temple of the household god. But there's no going back. Our homes lie in rubble. So we must face the desert demons. If we're to discover our true identity in the desert, they must be purged from our system, vomited up one by one under the blazing sun until we die in the spiritual emptiness Jesus astonishingly praises as the first and greatest of blessings. This cleansing unto death is a necessary prelude to heeding the dark and silent summons carried on the desert wind.

Falling in battle with the demons who haunt us is the second stage in the spiritual adventurer's journey toward God. Chapter 5 deals with the third stage, rebirth, and it is this book's centerpiece. In rooting out and slaying the demons of the pretender self, the desert God also slays our pre-wilderness identity. What remains is precisely nothing, a void, an emptiness, a pure openness utterly receptive to the divine emptiness, the holy silence, the great naught of the desert God. When our emptiness meets God's emptiness, an emptiness that paradoxically is also vibrant presence, we enter the mystical unity that is our destiny. We are reborn into our original image, propelled into the fusion with God that is the mystic's goal. The cocoon bursts open and the butterfly wings into the sun to become one with it.

But we've seen that the mystic is also a prophet, and the task of a prophet is to return. This is the final stage of the desert adventure, and it is treated in chapter 6. When we're reborn in the desert koan, we unite with the God of love and become infused with God's love. But the essence of love is a reaching-out to others in compassion and empathy. So the mystic-prophet goes back to the world she left to denounce household gods and prepare a path for the Lord. Like a Bodhisattva from the Buddhist tradition, she is restless until she coaxes all creation into the desert of purgative death and enlightened rebirth. When the desert-sojourner returns from her time of testing, then, she does so as a co-creator of the Kingdom of Heaven, charged by her wilderness experience to expand the reign of divine love until the entire cosmos is absorbed into the great koan of God.

Karl Rahner challenges us to go to the desert so that we may become the mystics and prophets we're intended to be. But the thought of taking on the mantle of mystic-prophet may seem too daunting for some. To those people, Rahner puts the same point in a different and perhaps less formidable way: We go to the desert in order to become *persons.*

> The real and total and comprehensive task of a Christian as a Christian is to be a human being, a human being of course whose depths are divine. These depths are inescapably present in his [or her] existence and open it outwards. And to this extent Christian life is the acceptance of human existence as such.[19]

This is the final and culminating truth whispered by the wilderness koan. We only become human beings, fully arrived persons, when we mystically touch base with the divinity that saturates our humanity and prophetically allow it to open outwards. This outward opening is the blossoming of the desert rose celebrated by the author of the Psalms of Solomon. And such flowers grow in one place only: the wilderness.

Chapter Two

Household Gods

Is the soul solid, like iron?
Or is it tender and breakable, like
the wings of a moth in the beak of the owl?
Mary Oliver

Blazing Novas, Cooling Stars

The twentieth-century novelist and essayist Yevgeny Zamyatin once wrote something that those of us who hesitate at the desert's edge would do well to heed. There are, he suggested, two basic and incompatible "laws" of the spirit: revolution on the one hand, entropy on the other. They reveal themselves in all arenas of human expression—science, politics, art, literature, fashion—but especially in religion. Whatever else can be said about the religious life, this much is certain: It's a constant pendulum swing between revolutionary heat and entropic chill.

When revolution is in the ascendancy, religious sensibility is like a blazing nova that "bursts into today from tomorrow." Explosive with a white-hot passion to lose herself to the desert God, the revolutionary religionist scorns comfortable dogma and easy answers. She welcomes the dreadful opportunity to be consumed by divine flame, knowing full well that only its scorching blast can melt a heart of ice. True, the fiery burst incinerates the old self. As Zamyatin says, "the law of revolution is red, fiery, deadly." But blasting away egoism, smugness, complacency, and spiritual sloth brings about "the birth of new life, a new star." The Pentecost event, Paul's strobe light encounter on the Damascus Road, John's apocalyptic visions—each are examples of the old self going nova, exploding into millions of fragments, and birthing new stars, new souls.[1]

But pitted against revolutionary ardor is the temptation to entropic religiosity, the compulsion to play it safe, to stick with the stolidly conventional. What once was "fiery magma" cools into a "rigid, ossified, motionless crust" that insulates us from scorching pentecostal flames. Religion becomes "cold, ice blue, like the icy interplanetary infinities. The flame turns from red to an even, warm pink, no longer deadly, but comfortable." When entropy overtakes the spirit, we harden into whited sepulchres: properly pious on the outside, hollow and lifeless—"comfortable"—on the inside. "Instead of the Sermon on the Mount, under the scorching sun, to up-raised arms and sobbing people, there is drowsy prayer in a magnificent abbey."[2]

Zamyatin's warning against entropic religiosity is nothing new. Similar ones crop up in every generation—understandably so, since entropy is an ever present temptation. Moses condemns the ice blue spirituality of haughty Pharaoh, Elijah that of the Baalites. The Hebrew prophets lament that their peers have reduced the fiery covenant with Yahweh to a mechanical quid pro quo arrangement. John the Baptist and Jesus blast both Pharisees and Sadducees for hypocritical smugness in spiritual matters. Paul warns Hellenistic philosophers that their indifferent nod of the head to the abstract (and hence safely distant) "unknown God" is spiritual cowardice. And the author of Revelation ominously tells the Laodicean church that the God who abominates entropy in faith will spew out tepid believers on the day of judgment.

Revelation's warning to lukewarm believers is just as relevant today as it was two millennia ago. In the minds of many observers, Christianity (at least in the northern hemisphere) started sliding into entropic ossification around the seventeenth century.[3] Although it's tempting to chalk up this modern cooling to the cold breath of science and secularization, such finger-pointing is too easy. What the Jewish theologian and mystic Abraham Heschel says about the entropic slide of religion in general is equally applicable to Christianity:

> Religion declined not because it was refuted, but because it became irrelevant, dull, oppressive, insipid. When faith is completely replaced by creed, worship by discipline, love by habit;...when faith becomes an heirloom rather than a living fountain...its message becomes meaningless.[4]

The sorry upshot of entropic religiosity is a smothering of that revolutionary fire in the belly that John the Baptist preached and Jesus exemplified. Christianity ceases to be a fireball of intensity that scandalizes and challenges and ultimately slays in order to rejuvenate. It loses both its mystical immediacy and its prophetic vision. When that happens, as Søren Kierkegaard chillingly observed, Christianity becomes "a nothing, a silly game, something...one slips into more easily than one slips into the most trifling accomplishment."[5] Thus, concludes Jacques Ellul, Kierkegaard's twentieth-century successor, is Christianity "subverted" from within. We find its deep message too unsettling—"grace is intolerable, the Father is unbearable, weakness is discouraging, freedom is unlivable, spiritualization is deceptive"—yet at the same time lack the courage for a complete break. So we ladle the waters of entropy on it until its white heat cools to a more comfortable temperature.[6]

For too many of us, Christianity has become the softly textured leisure suit Kierkegaard and Ellul condemn. This is our normal state, the spiritual place where we dwell. It is, in the vocabulary of the spiritual adventurer's journey, our "home." If we ever hope to progress toward our true destiny, we must leave home, the place of religious entropy, and venture into the revolutionary wilderness. We must exchange our satin robes for ones of coarse camel hair, forsaking the drowsy abbey for the mercilessly scorching desert sun.

Lares

It was the custom of ancient Romans to erect shrines to household gods, or *lares*. At first probably deified ancestors, *lares* eventually came to be seen as minor deities who lived in the home and ensured domestic tranquillity. Statues of *lares* were regularly garlanded and supplicated, and when a family moved to a new dwelling, its *lares,* guarantors of homey comforts, naturally went as well.

Lares were idols on two different counts. Most obviously, they were graven images worshipped and reverenced by householders. More significantly, they—like all idols—were safe substitutes for the fiery desert God. The *lares'* job wasn't to stoke spiritual flame or prod souls into the wilderness, but rather to sanctify the familiar coziness of home. Calm, comfort, unembarrassing conventionality, respectable moderation, material well-being—these were the ideals exemplified by *lares*. It was all very urbane.

We no longer pay homage to Roman *lares,* but we do have our own household gods who serve as domesticated stand-ins for the feral God of the desert. When we mistake these gods for the real thing, we chisel our spiritual homes out of the cooled magma of revolutionary ardor. In worshipping these false gods, we fancy ourselves safe from the hot desert breeze. We build cocoons for ourselves, but not at all with the intention of St. Teresa's silkworm. The silkworm voluntarily imprisons itself so that it may eventually soar on the back of God's wind. We encase ourselves in the cocoon of household gods so that the wind—liberating because fatal to spiritual coziness—will whistle safely outside. Little do we suspect that our cocoon-sanctuaries are flimsy structures indeed—that, as poet Elizabeth Bishop notes,

> My house, my fairy
>   palace, is
> of perishable
>   clapboards...[7]

The fairy palace we must forsake if we hope to find the wilderness-God is carved from many household deities, but there are four primary ones: the syllogistic god, the orgy-porgy god, the codex god, and the resumé god. Among them, these *lares* cover the range of safe havens in which we typically seek shelter from the desert. In this chapter we'll limit ourselves to their description, reserving for chapter 3 a critical analysis of why they, like all idols, eventually topple and shatter.

The Syllogistic God. Most of us dislike conceptual ambiguity. We crave precision and clarity in our beliefs as well as our judgments, and ambiguity only tosses us the bone of anxious uncertainty. To compound the injury, ambiguity also offends against the conceit that we "rational" creatures are able to use our intellects to understand, predict, and control events and situations. It threatens the empowering sense of self-determination we take as our birthright.

But the wilderness God is the ultimate ambiguity because, as koan, he is a paradox who forever defies our feeble efforts at intellectual definition and classification. This is one of the reasons a whiff of desert air unsettles the homebody. So some people, particularly those temperamentally drawn to the "life of the mind," compensate by paying homage to a household god who protects them from the discomfort of conceptual messiness. Their *lar,* the "syllogistic god," offers the intellectual precision they demand when it comes to thinking about things divine.

If John the Baptist is the archetypal worshipper of the desert God, a character out of Hermann Hesse's novel *Narcissus and Goldmund* typifies a devotee of the syllogistic god. Narcissus, one of the book's two eponymous protagonists, is an intensely cerebral medieval monk dedicated to the "service of the mind." He's a relentlessly "analytical thinker" who lives in an abstract world "made of ideas." Narcissus is doubly cloistered: first behind the stone and mortar walls of his abbey, second and more significantly behind the conceptual ones of his theology and philosophy. As Hesse puts it, "all was mind to him," and this "all" includes God. Narcissus' relationship to the Divine, like his relationship to everything else, is first and foremost as a thinker.[8]

Narcissus has chosen this enclosed existence because he deplores and fears the messy bogginess of raw, unfiltered experience. Just as monastic vocation rescues him from the everyday world's unpredictable exigencies, so the life of the mind, which "favors the definite," whisks him out of the swamp of conceptual ambiguity and into the pristinely sculptured garden of abstract thought.[9] Reason tames unruly experience by systematically plugging it into conceptually neat compartments impervious to the eroding effects of ambiguity. These compartments translate both the world and God into abstract language free from the taint of repellent mystery. The teeming world freezes into a coherent but static system of geometrical relations, the desert's blazing God ices over to become the frigidly abstract conclusion of a logical syllogism. This is the only deity Narcissus' hyper-intellectualism wants or can tolerate.

Like all exemplars, Narcissus is an extreme case in one sense but a representative one in another. His extremism lies in the fact that he, unlike most nonfictional worshippers of the syllogistic god, is explicitly aware of his compulsion to reduce the paradoxical desert God to the manageable status of a concept. But he's representative because many of us, particularly those attracted to philosophy and theology, likewise focus our attention more on an *idea* of God than on *God*.

This ideational quality is precisely the appeal of the syllogistic god. It's an object of abstract thought—an idea—rather than an existential encounter, and abstractions are both safe and satisfying. They're safe because we can bring them into sharp focus, conceptually tinkering with them until the ambiguity of a real encounter is eliminated. They're satisfying because they offer a continuous source of intellectual preoccupation, and also because we delude ourselves into supposing that our ideas accurately mirror the world. So focusing on logical abstractions rather than existential encounters both appeals to our native curiosity and gives us the comfortable sense of getting to the heart of things—and all without any real risk to ourselves.

A worshipper of the syllogistic god thus elevates his desire for safety and satisfaction to a virtue. His psychological need to escape the marsh of ambiguity leads him to the conclusion that any idea worth taking seriously must pass the Cartesian litmus test of absolute clarity and distinctness. The more important the idea under scrutiny, the more imperative the need for reason's light to render it transparent. Since the idea of God is ultimately important, the primary religious duty of the believer is to be clear about what he accepts and worships. Anything less is unworthy of a devotee of the syllogistic god. Anything less allows the rank swamp weeds of superstition, folk religion, and magic to crop up.

Because the worshipper of the syllogistic god focuses on an idea of God rather than God, he typically expresses his reverence by systematically formulating rational "proofs" for the existence of God. This, of course, is consistent with his conviction that beliefs are legitimate only if they can be logically justified. In the history of western theology and philosophy, such justifications run the gamut from purely conceptual ones to those that claim to be logical deductions from phenomena observed in the natural world. But they all operate from the assumption that God is the conclusion of syllogistic reasoning, not an irreducible mystery.

The predictable upshot of worshipping a purely conceptual god is that religious belief becomes disassociated from the fiery realm of encounter. The syllogistic god can be thought, and thought in elaborately technical ways. But it can't be lived and breathed or loved and embraced. These are responses proper to experiences, not to abstractions. We never drop to our knees in front of ideas; the most we can do with them is marvel at their conceptual sophistication or admire their logical clarity. But for the person who follows Narcissus' way, this substitution of arid thought for pulsating encounter is entirely palatable. The syllogistic god, icily immaculate in his logical dress, may not speak to an aching heart, but neither does he scorch or kill. For Narcissus and his tribe, the trade-off is a good one.

The Orgy-Porgy God. Devotees of the syllogistic god protect themselves from the desert sirocco by substituting an abstract idea for a living encounter with divine mystery. But the immaculate aerie they build in the thin atmosphere of pure thought isn't for everyone. Other people, equally wary of the wilderness, are temperamentally inclined more toward gushiness than logical abstractions. They're spiritually at home only in the hothouse of oceanic emotions and feel-good sentimentality. These combustible individuals worship a different *lar,* the "orgy-porgy god."

The name of this household deity is taken from Aldous Huxley's imaginative description of the pseudo-religious "Solidarity Service" in his novel *Brave New World.* The inhabitants of Huxley's futuristic society worship an amorphous deity named "Ford," and they meet twice a week in apostolically numbered groups of twelve to pay him homage. Anticipation runs high at the Solidarity Service: Each worshipper eagerly awaits the "mystical" coming of Ford, a descent of the "holy spirit" that for a short time allows them "to be fused, to lose their twelve separate identities in a larger being."[10]

Everything in the service is geared toward this ecstatic fusion. Synthetic music punctuated by "the soft indefatigable beating of drums" loosens up the worshippers. As they sway to the hypnotic drumbeat they solemnly pass around a loving cup of soma, the brave new world's drug of choice. Each member takes the cup, intones "I drink to my annihilation," and quaffs.

Twelve times the loving cup passes from hand to hand, accompanied by the steadily increasing tempo of the music. Expectancy stretches tauter and tauter. Excitement builds. Personal worries dissolve. Inhibitions fly away. The worshippers experience a "sensation of warmth" which "thrillingly" radiates "to every extremity" of their bodies. Tears flood their eyes; they quiver, they moan, and as the drum rhythm picks up and the soma flows through their blood, they feel the electric approach of our Ford. Eventually someone ecstatically shouts "I hear him!" Then the twelve jump to their feet. This is the signal they've awaited. Intoxicated by the presence of their god, they frenziedly caper in a rumba-like way about the room.

> Round they went, a circular procession of dancers, each with hands on the hips of the dancer preceding, round and round, shouting in unison, stamping to the rhythm of the music with their feet, beating it, beating it out with hands on the buttocks in front; twelve pairs of hands beating as one; as one, twelve buttocks slabbily resounding. Twelve as one, twelve as one.[11]

The music reels ever more intensely, the dance gyrates ever more feverishly, and the twelve disciples, now whipped to near "dissolving" point, break into dithyrambic chant:

> *Orgy-porgy, Ford and fun,*
> *Kiss the girls and make them One.*
> *Boys at one with girls at peace;*
> *Orgy-porgy gives release.*[12]

The longed for crescendo of twelve-in-one and one-in-twelve is immediate: Afire with the presence of the "greater being," the worshippers throw themselves on a thoughtfully provided ring of couches and copulate with uninhibited, lascivious—but sanctified— abandon. Afterward, they depart with "the calm ecstasy of achieved consummation."[13] All praise to our Ford!

The Solidarity Service is a parody, of course, and like all parodies it brings home an unpleasant truth. Huxley's targets here aren't the Eucharist or the mystical ideal of unification with God, but rather their perversions by devotees of the orgy-porgy god. Like the syllogistic god, its polar opposite, the Solidarity Service's *lar* is a refuge from the hazards of genuine encounter. The first god offers a haven against the desert sun by insulating the worshipper in layer upon layer of ideas; the second one protects by submerging the worshipper in a tidal wave of intense and self-absorbed sensual pleasure. The first reduces God to the status of a deductive argument's conclusion; the other reduces God to pure emotion. The final purpose of the orgy-porgy "eucharist" is a dissolving of one's identity in a whirlwind of sensation, an emotional and bodily ecstasy so like sexual climax that, once achieved, the worshipper collapses in post-coital lassitude.

Real-life worshippers of the orgy-porgy god may not actually couple in bacchanalian frenzy, but they're as completely addicted to intense emotion and self-referential sensuality as their brave new world counterparts. Their god is an experience—but an experience, unlike the desert encounter with God, that is always and everywhere pleasurably thrilling and safely choreographed.

Obviously there are gradations in the pleasure's intensity: Sometimes the orgy-porgy god is merely a warm, feel-good consolation, sometimes a raggedly explosive orgasm that convulses the whole body. But whatever the level, the sanctuary from distress or unhappiness or despair offered by the orgy-porgy god is pleasure. An ocean of good feeling whose tide sweeps us away from ourselves and our troubles—this is the bottom line boon the orgy-porgy *lar* bestows. And it's a gift that's especially welcome because, like the aftermath of sex, we always return to ourselves, sated but with our identities intact, ready to take on the world again until the tension builds to the point where we need another release.

The worshipper of the syllogistic god insists that the only true religiosity is one that operates from a clear and distinct idea of the Divine. The worshipper of the orgy-porgy god likewise has a written-in-stone litmus test, and it's the experience of ecstatic satiety. God isn't truly adored until a person achieves a spiritual climax whose pleasure is so intense that it mimics orgasmic abandonment. Anything short of this crescendo—which can range from unabashed outbursts like speaking in tongues or snake handling to more genteel but equally gushy displays of religious aestheticism (much less dark episodes of outright spiritual pain or desolation or fear)—is peremptory verification of a lack of faith.

The Codex God. Some people are as temperamentally inclined toward clarity and precision as worshippers of the syllogistic god, but have little use or talent for abstruse philosophical speculation. So they seek haven in a deity who reveals himself in clear and precise laws that disallow ambiguity or exception. Their god is the cosmic codifier, the celestial bookkeeper whose eagle-eye meticulously observes, records, and judges every human action. Devotion to this divine lawgiver is measured in terms of lockstep conformity to his commandments. The logical hair-splitting of the syllogistic god and the oceanic emotional intensity of the orgy-porgy one isn't for these people. They worship instead the *lar* of the "codex."

We may turn to the New Testament's depiction of the Pharisees for an illustration of the codex god devotee. Like the examples drawn from Hesse and Huxley, this is a fictional one. We now know that the early church's portrait of the Pharisees is a caricature rather than an historically accurate description.[14] But no matter. We're searching here for illustrations of a *type* of false spirituality, and fictional ones serve the purpose just as well as factual ones.

The three synoptic gospelists especially press home the allegiance of the Pharisees to the codex god. Matthew, Mark, and Luke all portray them as religionists obsessed with making sure that the purity of traditional law is rigorously observed down to the slightest jot and tittle. Their god is a jealous god who brooks no transgressions, and the duty of a devotee is to watchdog himself and others with unrelenting vigilance. According to the gospelists, what infuriated the Pharisees most about Jesus was his casual disregard of the hundreds of rules and regulations, commandments and prohibitions, prescribed by the divine legislator. Such a flaunting of the codex was nothing less than blasphemy (cf. Matt 36:65, Mark 2:7), because the elaborately detailed system of law was taken by the Pharisees to be the unassailable word of the Lord.

So the Pharisees do their best to trip up Jesus and his followers. *You and your disciples do what isn't lawful on the Sabbath!* They rage again and again. *You're collecting food, you're working!* Or: *You and your disciples transgress the tradition of the elders because you don't wash your hands before you eat!* Or: *You and your disciples violate the laws of purity because you associate with unclean persons!* Or: *You instruct your disciples to stretch beyond the ten commandments in their quest for spiritual purity! But purity comes only from strict compliance to Torah!*

Because the Jesus of the gospels gave as good as he got and vigorously condemned the Pharisees for their lockstep shallowness, it's easy for Christians to dismiss them as rather stupid fanatics who mindlessly substituted the letter of the law for its spirit. But we should look for the mote in our own eyes, because the allure of the codex god is incredibly strong even for those of us today who pityingly shake our heads at such rigidity. We may pooh-pooh specific points of law insisted on by first-century Pharisees—dietary or sartorial prohibitions, for example—but many of us nonetheless crave a god who tells us exactly what to do and what not to do. We have the uneasy suspicion that humans would run amok and society collapse into chaos without clear-cut guidelines to dictate behavior. The contemporary worshipper of the codex god can laugh at the quaintness of legal prohibitions in Deuteronomy or Leviticus and still be quite willing to legalistically invoke his favorite scriptural rule at every available opportunity.

It's not surprising that devotees of the codex god tend to be literalists in religious and ethical matters (even if they *are* somewhat selective in their choice of texts). Not for them ambiguous interpretations or extenuating circumstances that leave open the possibility of deviation from the letter of the law. Commandments and prohibitions are the once-and-for-all revealed word of God, and that word must be taken at face value. Any suggestion that scripture can be read on different levels to accommodate a number of viable points of view is too confusing for the faithful and unworthily obtuse of the supreme lawmaker. So what if a particular law seems unreasonable? The

value of the codex stems from the fact that it exhaustively cata-
logues all necessary regulations and requirements, not that it
provides justification for them. The codex god doesn't care if
humans actually comprehend his mandates. Like all lawmak-
ers, he demands one thing only: unquestioning obedience. His
ways are not our ways, and we only make trouble for ourselves
if we try to second-guess him.

John Stuart Mill once remarked that there are two personality types in the world: those who crave the challenge of creative freedom, the hazardous thrill of an open-ended future,
and those who desire nothing more than a safely predictable
existence in which the future is determined for them by
someone else.[15] Mill's typology is an over-simplification, but
it's certainly the case that disciples of the codex god are more
predisposed toward conformity to set-in-stone tradition than
to an open-ended and hence risky spirituality. The furniture
in their religious home must be so immaculately arranged
that they always know the precise whereabouts of every
item. Even in the darkest night there's no danger of stubbing
a toe because everything is exactly where the codex inventory
says it ought to be. Worship becomes a matter of undeviating
schedules, granite routines, and liturgical habit. Righteousness is defined by fidelity to an inflexible list of dos and
don'ts. There's no need for making a decision, because everything has already been spelled out once and for all in the
recipe book of the codex. And that book allows no leeway.
Recipes must be followed exactly as they're written.

The Resumé God. Different household gods hunger for
different burnt offerings. The syllogistic god's nostrils twitch
in delight at the alpine purity of logic, the orgy-porgy god
basks in the heat of unbridled emotionality, and the codex

god loves nothing more than row upon row of neatly-bound regulation books. The fourth *lar,* the "resumé god," is indifferent to each of these offerings. What pleases him is an energetic curriculum vitae. He likes go-getters.

Father Urban, the lead character in J. F. Powers' novel *Morte d'Urban,* is an exemplary go-getter and thus a good illustration of the resumé god devotee. A priest in the fictional Order of St. Clement, a rather bedraggled and bumbling outfit that barely manages to keep its head above water, Urban sees himself as just the "fighting general" to whip his fellow Clementines into shape and lead them to glory.[16] He has little patience with those Christians who sit on their hands mumbling prayers and devotions when there are victories to be won—and there are *always* victories to be won by the stout-hearted. Novitiates must be recruited, tons of money raised in whirlwind cross-country trips ("Frankly," Father Urban says of his order, "I think we're overstating the case for poverty"[17]), retreat centers built. In short, busyness—which for Urban usually translates into "business"—is the cardinal spiritual virtue. The problem is that too many people (including clergy, who after all ought to know better) would rather gripe about what needs to be done instead of rolling up their sleeves and getting down to business.

But not Father Urban. For him, what counts is "not running off the mouth at every opportunity, but knowing when to cast one's pearls, and how—that, in the best sense of the word, was priestcraft."[18] So Urban, good fighting general that he is, "stumped the country, preaching retreats and parish missions, and did the work of a dozen men"[19]—as well as, incidentally, schmoozing with wealthy benefactors, financial consultants, and savvy promoters. Urban must be about his Father's business, and that means keeping busy, always on the move, never stopping for a breather regardless of how well deserved it might be. At the end of the workday, when the tired company man stands before the celestial board of directors, the pension plan awarded him will be determined by the length of the resumé he can hand over.

Devotees of the resumé god have no time for impractical theologizing, and emotional outbursts are foolish expenditures of energy that could be put to better use. Nor do they feel constrained by the rigid regulations of the codex god. Getting the job done sometimes means bending the rules a bit, especially when there's so little time and so much to do. God's business, like all business, properly takes its cue from the bottom line. Everything else is secondary.

That bottom line, as the example of Urban shows, is unceasing busyness in pursuit of "good works." Those who take the resumé god as their *lar* generally cash out their allegiance in one of two ways: they identify God's business with the church's business, or they obsessively run around strewing indiscriminate acts of personal charity. In either case, what counts for them is quantity: how many church committees served on, how much bazaar money raised, how many new congregants added to the church roll, how many old ladies helped across the street, how much time put in at the soup kitchen or food bank. Every good work adds a new line to one's curriculum vitae. It rarely occurs to the Urbans of the world that quality might be more essential than quantity, that they're spreading themselves too thin to perform well, or that spiritual intent is just as important as actual deed.

Their blind spot is partly temperamental, but it also stems from the fact that the frenetic race to build a strong resumé leaves them with little or no time to reflect on their own motives. Busyness has a way of shielding us from a self-scrutiny that can reveal unpleasant truths about our reasons for doing what we do. By immersing ourselves in the frantic race to get things done, we conveniently bypass considerations of why and focus exclusively on what. And once we cross over into the realm of whats, the only thing that matters is accomplishment. I *am* my tote sheet, my per capita production, my vitae, and my worth is proportionate to how many whats I achieve. If the home sought by the devotee of the codex god is one where every stick of furniture has its designated and proper spot, the home of the resumé god disciple is crammed from floor to ceiling with achievement awards and letters of commendation for jobs well done.

Still, there *is* a common bond between the codex god and the resumé god: Both value efficiency. Undeviating conformity to inflexible coda guarantees regularity in human behavior and minimizes the risk of sloppy individualism: equally necessary conditions for running an efficient ship. Similarly, designing a game plan of good works and then vigorously following through with it until the desired objectives are reached, whether those objectives are institutional (a church fundraiser) or personal (a scorecard filled with charitable acts), is the hallmark of resumé efficiency. Mary may sit mooning at the feet of Jesus, but it's Martha who sees what has to be done, puts on her apron, and gets to work. And when it comes right down to it, which is more important: daydreaming or baking bread? For the worshippers of the resumé god, the answer is obvious.

Gods of Iron

Most household shrines tend to become cluttered over time. Moods swing, needs emerge, desires compound, and new *lares* are added to meet these changes in circumstance.

Accordingly, it's entirely possible for our spiritual homes to contain two or more incompatible gods at different stages of our lives. It's as if there's a spiritual pendulum effect at work here. The atmosphere of abstraction occasionally becomes so oppressively thin that the syllogistic god disciple takes a holiday by throwing himself at the more robust feet of the resumé god. The codexer's rigid fidelity to objective rules and regulations sometimes grows so confining that he bursts out in an orgy-porgy reaction of uninhibited emotionalism.

Still, as we've seen, people normally gravitate to the gods they worship because of psychological predisposition. A spiritual home is where we feel most comfortable, and our idea of comfort is fundamentally determined by temperament. The pendulum effect may occasionally bounce us back and forth, but most of us have a dispositional center of gravity to which we eventually return, a primary *lar* to whom we come back. The temperamental thinker remains more or less loyal to the syllogistic god; the gusher to the orgy-porgy god; the legalist to the codex god; and the go-getter to the resumé god.

What is it that each person finds comforting in the primary household god he or she worships? Our examination of the four *lares* has already suggested an answer: the entropic longing for spiritual safety. This point is grippingly conveyed in a remarkable autobiographical fragment in which Pierre Teilhard de Chardin recounts his earliest spiritual experience.

Teilhard tells us that as a child he obsessively collected his own set of household gods. These *lares* all had one thing in common: they were made of metal. Any metallic object—a discarded plough-spanner, a bit of iron rod, spent shells from a firing range—became a powerful symbol of divinity for the boy. Describing his youthful religiosity to an acquaintance years later, Teilhard wrote:

> You should have seen me as in profound secrecy and silence I withdrew into the contemplation of my "God of Iron," delighting in its possession, gloating over its existence. A God, note, of iron; and why iron? Because in all my childish experience there was nothing in the world harder, tougher, more durable than this wonderful substance.[20]

Teilhard's disarming confession clearly illustrates the need for safety that motivates fidelity to household gods. But it also hints at a startling new twist: Part of the reason *lares* are safe is because they, unlike the desert God, can be manipulated by their worshippers. The desert God is wild, unpredictable, darkly primordial; iron gods aren't. We can hold them in our hands, turn them this way and that. We can *know* them, and knowledge is power.

Such controllable gods immediately bring to mind religious fetishism. A fetish, of course, is a talisman believed to possess the magical ability to protect its owner from danger. A fetish may be a natural object (a stone, feather, or curiously shaped root), an artifactual one (a statue, doll, or amulet), or a combination of the two (a rabbit's foot key chain). But regardless of how it's made, a fetish always serves one purpose: to protect its holder from life's exigencies. The world is fraught with unpredictable dangers over which the hapless individual has no control. Nothing is reliable; nothing is guaranteed. A fetish provides safe passage because it radiates ju-ju tough and durable enough to withstand any onslaught. The fetish-worshipper is safe so long as he keeps the fetish securely in his possession.

Teilhard delightedly gloated over his god of iron because, like all fetishes, it was a bulwark against the things that frightened him. True, his fears were boyish ones: loss of parental approval, failure in school, rained-out holidays, and so on. But fear is fear, regardless of its context or justification. It causes suffering, and all suffering cries to be alleviated. What better remedy than a god of iron? Iron is an incredibly strong substance that resists blows, changes in climate, and pressure. A god of iron is hard enough to weather life's ambiguities and unpredictable mishaps—and, above all, to stand up against the windstorms that blow in from the desert. A god of iron encases us in a suit of armor that wards off doubt and ambiguity. Sometimes the armor's tough and durable stuff is forged from logic or emotion, sometimes from rule-conformity or busyness. Any material will do so long as it's iron-hard and iron-safe.

All these advantages are obvious. But as I said, iron gods are also attractive because they provide another kind of security secretly desired but rarely owned up to by their devotees: They can be manipulated to serve human needs and desires. For all its toughness, iron is malleable. Human ingenuity can forge it into any number of instruments, bend it into dozens of useful shapes and sizes especially made to suit our purposes. It's revealing that many of the fetishes collected by Teilhard were utensils: plough-spanners, spent shells, factory rods. When we worship household gods, we take unto ourselves deities who are eminently usable. They are practical tools and efficient weapons; we are the tool-users and the weapon-wielders. In pledging ourselves to iron gods, we make them pledge to us as well, bidding them iron-clad our souls and house us in cocoons of undisturbable entropy.

— 43 —

When we slip into the winter of entropy, our souls become sluggish, freezing into inert things as the temperature drops. A soul complacently frozen in place requires a spirituality that reflects and encourages its turgidity. So it turns to gods every bit as immobile and thing-like as it is, gods that are ready-to-hand objects rather than dangerously ineluctable mysteries. Objects are easily definable and readily controllable. They never surprise us and, above all, they never threaten. Their primary function is to make life easier. Thus the syllogistic god is a thought-object that massages our intellectual pride; the orgy-porgy god is a sensation-object that indulges our need to let off emotional steam; the codex god is a slide-rule-object that conveniently calculates moral choices for us; and the resumé god is an agenda-object that writes our daily routine. Protected by this iron pantheon, which makes no demands on us and is always at our beck and call, we build spiritual homes for ourselves filled with the latest in household appliances, homes that are cozy, satisfying, convenient, and above all burglar-proof.

Or so we think. But as the poet Mary Oliver suggests, the soul is never truly ironclad. It is "tender and breakable," and this guarantees that it won't bear up under the cold weight of the iron gods it worships and foolishly seeks to command. The soul—the heart—is made to rise:

> The human heart—what is it for?
> Cosmic temperature. Heart. Mercury.[21]

Chapter Three

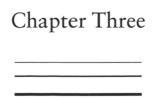

At Desert's Edge

Clearly it is time
To become disillusioned, each person to
enter his own soul's desert
And look for God—having seen man.
Robinson Jeffers

Rusted Iron

Sooner or later, homebodies run up against the sobering fact that iron corrodes. Sometimes this truth dawns suddenly and shockingly, but usually it's more gradual. As the years go by we uneasily start to notice flaws in our iron gods. The cracks can be ignored only so long; eventually even the most stubborn fetishist must admit there's a problem.

So it happened with the youthful Teilhard de Chardin. He paid homage to the god of iron for several years—for as long as he possibly could—until the bleak moment when he had to acknowledge his fairy palace as the illusion it was. "I can never forget the pathetic depths of a child's despair," he wrote, "when I realised one day that iron can be scratched and can rust. I had to look elsewhere for substitutes that would console me."[1]

We homebodies only venture into the desert when forced to confess that the household we've grown accustomed to is no fit place to dwell, and we only come to that reluctant conclusion when the weight of our *lares* finally becomes too burdensome to endure. The homey comfort we sought from them reveals itself as entrapment; our safe havens mutate into prison cells; our smug sense of being in charge is recognized as the wishful thinking of a slave. The god of iron rusts. But what else could we have expected? All objects—even deified ones—decay.

Abraham Heschel warned that religion sinks into entropy when it becomes "irrelevant, dull, oppressive, insipid." These negative qualities are the four kinds of rust that eat away at our household deities. The syllogistic god eventually succumbs to dullness; the orgy-porgy god to insipidity; the codex god to oppressiveness; and the resumé god to irrelevance.

Dullness. When we worship the syllogistic god, we forsake the heart for the head. Frightened by the mystery of the desert and the messiness of experience, we retreat into a sanctuary of bloodless logic and frigid abstraction. Like Narcissus, we want nothing to do with an unfathomable God who stubbornly remains hidden. The only deity we desire is one who can be pegged down by pure thought—a God, says Merton, whom we can "confine…within the limits" of a clear idea.[2] So we spin philosophical theories and contrive theological arguments in order to vanquish ambiguity and demystify mystery. We secure ourselves against the existential bogginess that troubled Narcissus, and we acquire power over our iron god by locking him in a conceptual framework of our own making.

But the opportunity cost of this is a god so abstract, so aloof, so antiseptically removed from the unsanitary world in which we live, that he's vacuously uninspiring and boringly dull. What the soul truly hungers for in its deepest, most secret core is to be swept off its feet by the living God, and dead abstractions just don't generate this kind of jolt. We can't relate personally to ideas; we only observe them. We can't enter into intimacy with theories; we only tinker with them. Metaphysical proofs for the existence of God don't flame up like burning bushes to consume us. They only radiate a moon-cold nimbus. This may be enough to satisfy the head, but the heart is forever frustrated by such lackluster dullness. The heart throbs for the blazing yet ineluctable God of Abraham and Sarah, a God who sets us trembling under the desert sun with awe and fear and adoration. That throbbing is primary, while conceptual models are always secondary. Even the most eminent theologian of our day admits that a sincere cry of longing from the heart is "more significant" than all the "learned talk" and "theological language" in the world.[3]

As we saw in chapter 2, the fundamental error made by the devotee of the syllogistic god is to mistake her ideas *about* God *for* God. This is an example of what the philosopher Alfred North Whitehead called the "fallacy of misplaced concreteness." We run afoul of the fallacy when we become so fixated on abstract theories and arguments that we confuse them with the reality they're intended to map. A corollary of this "misplacement" of theory for reality is that we also "fall into a false estimate of logical procedure" by presuming that any belief resistant to the canons of logic is necessarily suspect and not worth taking seriously.[4] Such idea-olatry dismisses mystery as confusion and refuses to acknowledge any spiritual experience that doesn't square with an abstract formulation of God. The devotee of the syllogistic god locks himself into a theory that may be immaculate, but only because it's utterly removed from the sharply vibrant "concreteness" of a genuine encounter with the divine. As Dame Julian warned in the fourteenth century, "The more we busy ourselves to know [God's] secrets now in this, now in the other, the further shall we be from knowing them."[5]

None of this is to say that the God-seeker should dismiss logical precision or rational thinking out of hand. But it does caution against the arrogant presumption that our intellects can exhaustively explain God, or that we can substitute thinking about God for experiencing God. When we try to box the desert wind in an airtight syllogism, we sacrifice awe for erudition, intimacy for understanding, and an openness to experience for self-enclosed staticity. The consequence is a household god whose dullness eventually imprisons the spirit. Reflecting on his own years of homage to the syllogistic god, Merton rued the trap he'd fallen into:

> But, oh, how blind and weak and sick I was, although I thought I saw where I was going, and half understood the way! How deluded we sometimes are by the clear notions we get out of books. They make us think that we really understand things of which we have no practical knowledge at all. I remember how learnedly and enthusiastically I could talk for hours about mysticism and the experimental knowledge of God....[6]

Rather than take this risk, we are better served to follow the way of the Zen master Hsiang-yen Chi-hsien. For years the learned Hsiang-yen paid homage to the syllogistic god, convinced that elaborate theorizing about the Divine would eventually force God to reveal his face. But one day a flash of *satori* shoved Hsiang-yen headlong into the unfathomable mystery of the desert, and he instantly came to know the dull lifelessness of his philosophical god. He immediately burnt his books and manuscripts. "Rice cakes in a picture," he said, "do not satisfy one's hunger."[7]

Insipidity. When we pay homage to the syllogistic god, we allow the intellect's Apollonian drive for logical clarity to freeze the heart. But when we cleave to the orgy-porgy god, we invite a Dionysian tidal wave of passion to wash away reason. Orgy-porgy spirituality is a creature of the id, fueled by a frantic craving for sensual gratification and emotional release. Sometimes it settles for the artsy thrill of incense, stained glass, vaulted ceilings, and music. At other times only a sky-rocketing religious climax will do. But in either case, what it demands of God is a breathlessly ecstatic yet no-risk moment of pleasure.

Testimony throughout the centuries assures us that sometimes a genuine experience of the divine indeed is a sudden eruption of such sweet intensity that the soul swoons with pleasure. But tradition also warns against falling into the delusion that *all* God-encounters fit this pattern. An experience of God can just as well be terrifying, dreadful, violently bone-shaking. Moreover, not every moment of swooning emotional ecstasy is necessarily God-inspired: It's no accident that Huxley's brave new worlders achieve their "mystical" fusion through drugs and sex. That's why spiritual teachers such as Teresa d'Avila and John of the Cross again and again warn their readers against the danger of taking intense experiences of "sweet consolation" too seriously—first because they're unreliably duplicitous, second because they're addictive.[8]

They're also catalysts for hubris. The syllogistic god devotee reveals his arrogance by attempting to confine God in a theoretical formula spun from her intellect. The orgy-porgy-ist has no interest in conceptually imprisoning God, but he does demand that the deity be on call, ready and willing to provide an ecstatic *frisson* whenever it's wanted. The orgy-porgy devotee is a stage manager who carefully arranges theatrical opportunities for God's performances. A Huxleyian soma ceremony, a revivalist tent meeting, or a high church performance of Handel's "Messiah"—each is a choreographed "happening" in which God is under contract to do his shtick for gushing fans.

In the long run, this stage-crafted mania for intense emotional charges falls into a destructive spin. The orgy-porgyist is what Kierkegaard called an "aesthete," an individual consumed with craving for immediate sensual and emotional gratification.[9] Since he feels fully alive only in moments of ecstasy (one of the reasons they're addictive), he directs all his energy to sustaining them.

But the gratification sought by the religious aesthete is necessarily episodic and transitory. Gushy overflows can't continue indefinitely, and there's an inevitable let-down after the climax has passed. So the orgy-porgyist, hooked as he is on "sweet consolations," contrives ever new scenarios for the coming of the great Ford, and traps himself in a pernicious cycle: ecstasy followed by uneasiness followed by an increasingly frenetic scramble for new stage directions. Ingenuity eventually wears thin, and the opportunities for gushing choreographed by the orgy-porgyist take on a tastelessly insipid character, becoming either banally sentimental or boorishly vaudevillian. Moreover, the interludes between these insipidly tawdry moments become more frequent and last longer, propelling the aesthete into a chronic state of boredom alternating with frustration.

The law of diminishing returns that bedevils the religious gusher is a risk even in the *Brave New World*. Bernard, one of the Solidarity Service participants, goes into the ceremony with high expectations only to leave with a jaded sense of his own hollowness:

> He was as miserably isolated now as he had been when the service began—more isolated by reason of his unreplenished emptiness, his dead satiety. Separate and unatoned..., more hopelessly himself than he had ever been in his life before.... He was utterly miserable.[10]

It's with good reason, then, that Merton repeats for contemporary ears the warning of Teresa and John:

> Place no hope in the feeling of assurance, in spiritual comfort. You may well have to get along without this. Place no hope in the inspirational preachers of Christian sunshine, who are able to pick you up and set you back on your feet and make you feel good for three or four days—until you fold up and collapse into despair.[11]

Oppressiveness. Followers of the syllogistic and orgy-porgy gods are die-hard subjectivists. The spiritual homes they build for themselves are internal: intellect in the one case, pleasurable sensation and intense emotions in the other. Devotees of the codex and resumé gods go to the opposite extreme. They're unbending objectivists who insist on dwelling externally. If syllogistic and orgy-porgy disciples suffer from an excess of interiority, codex and resumé disciples are afflicted by an atrophy of interiority.

In the last chapter we saw that codexers above all want their deity to be a supreme bookkeeper who not only lays down unbending laws but also punishes infractions and rewards compliance with clockwork finesse. In their minds, the codex god *is* the sum total of rules and regulations that govern human behavior, and devotion to him is measured by how well those rules and regulations are obeyed and enforced. On the surface, this kind of spirituality appears self-effacing and subservient: The codexer subordinates his will (and insists that others do likewise) to the divine lawmaker's. But appearances are deceptive, because what appears to be subordination is a masked attempt to control God.

The reduction of deity to a hidebound set of rules tames the unpredictably feral God of the desert just as surely as syllogistic compartmentalizing and orgy-porgy choreographing do. Divine will is chained between the covers of a law book, and whatever one needs to know about God can be discovered by flipping to the appropriate paragraph, section, and subsection. In making this move, the codex devotee ties God's hands. The supreme lawmaker becomes as hamstrung by his laws as humans are. He cannot deviate from them in even the slightest way. Divine majesty and omnipotence—and, most of all, mercy—give way to stiff legalistic propriety. God *must* reward those who overtly conform to the rules, regardless of how twisted or broken their motives might be, just as he *must* punish those who fail to obey, regardless of the presence of extenuating circumstances or noble intentions. Outward conformity to the Law, the Code, is all that counts. Internal rectitude is, at best, secondary.

Snug and secure as a home constructed from law books might seem, it's actually a dungeon that sooner or later oppresses the human spirit. People are not automatons; we cannot flourish under a totalitarian regimen that prescribes lockstep fidelity to rules that exhaustively spell out exterior behavior while ignoring interior states. To be a human is to be what the philosopher Gabriel Marcel called *homo viator,* a wanderer—a *habiru*—continuously striving to break out of the cloying here-and-now toward the transcendent God. When we stymie the soul's freedom for the sake of safe conformity, we deny our natures and run the risk of pharisaic hypocrisy or religious pedantry. In the first case, we become whited sepulchres, respectably righteous on the outside but carrion-filled on the inside. In the second case, we go through life memorizing coda and mechanically parsing fine points of the law. Either alternative is crushingly oppressive because it does violence to our spiritual freedom for the sake of sanctimonious conformity to the dead letter of the law.

Nicodemus, the first-century pharisaic leader, dimly sensed after a conversation with Jesus (John 3:1–21) the exorbitant cost of worshipping the codex *lar:* a soul weighted down by accounting ledgers and legal scrolls, trapped within a maze of laws so torturously complex that the best legal mind in the world couldn't help overlooking a regulation every now and then. Nicodemus came to realize that the iron god of the codex makes spirituality burdensome rather than light, inevitably oppressing devotees with a helpless sense of inadequacy and failure.

Centuries later, the Baal Shem Tov, founder of Hasidism, arrived at the same conclusion. The European Jewish community, he decided, had bound itself to earth, mumbling and moiling over the *halakah* for so many generations that the secret of spiritual flight—adoration supersedes mindless legalism and freedom takes precedence over conformity to regulatory minutiae—had been forgotten. By fettering themselves to the law, the Baal Shem feared his fellow Jews had forfeited the Kingdom of Heaven. His disciple, Menahem Mendl of Kotzk, made the same point. Either one lives in awe of the Lord, he said, or in fear of the Code of Law. The first liberates; the second oppresses.[12]

Irrelevance. Like their codex cousins, worshippers of the resumé god focus on externalities to the exclusion of interior states. But unlike codexers, resumé devotees aren't sticklers for rules. They pride themselves on being realistic and practical, doers, active livers, good workers, and have little time or patience for laborious study of arcane law books. Neither does their god. He's a robust go-getter himself, and serving him means imitating his busyness. So the Father Urbans of the world scramble to "do good."

Resumé-ers work hard at doing good, often generously sacrificing their immediate personal interests for the sake of achieving their ends. They rarely run the risk of hypocrisy or pedantry that haunts codexers. Unhappily, however, their frenetic altruism is really a defense mechanism against the desert God. He can only be met in silence and stillness, solitude and quiet; but those who follow the resumé deity insist on seeing God as a bundle of nervous energy who both exemplifies and mandates ceaseless activity. They thereby insulate themselves against the frighteningly mysterious silence of God and the parallel silence that lies in their own hearts. Go-getters are too preoccupied with resumé building to be alone with either themselves or God.

All followers of iron gods seek a deity who can be manipulated, and resumé-ers are no exception. Their *lar* can be bargained with and bribed. The resumé god is a business man—the "everlasting Wanamaker," as D. H. Lawrence bitingly noted[13]—who's perfectly willing to cut a deal for the sake of the bottom line. Regardless of how spiritually hollow a person may be inside, he can still buy the resumé god's approval by presenting a sufficiently long tote sheet of "good" accomplishments.

The fly in the ointment is that the robust pursuit of external credentials doesn't impress the desert God. The hallowing of the soul, not the accumulation of triumphs, is the true goal of the spiritual life. Interior housecleaning is always a necessary prerequisite for exterior repair. But since the follower of the resumé god avoids diving into his own depths by scrambling to get things done in the world, he misses the whole point of good works. Distracted as he is with what Kierkegaard scornfully referred to as "bustling spiritual and worldly expedients," he fails to see his rushing around for what it is: a colossal irrelevancy.[14] This isn't to say that either Kierkegaard or any other spiritual teacher thinks good works ought not be pursued, but rather that good works without right intention are relatively meaningless. And right intention is founded on the cultivation of an interior life.

In the fourteenth century, the mystic Johannes Tauler preached against the irrelevance of a resumé spirituality. "What negotiations and occupations continually distract and absorb the world!" he exclaimed. "It would be better to die of hunger on the way than to allow ourselves to be encumbered by so many needless occupations."[15] Thomas Merton also deplored the resumé god worshippers' misguided willingness to allow themselves to be "devoured by activities and strangled with attachments."

> Interior solitude is impossible for them. They fear it. They do everything they can to escape it. What is worse, they try to draw everyone else into activities as senseless and as devouring as their own. They are great promoters of useless work. They love to organize meetings and banquets and conferences and lectures. They print circulars,

write letters, talk for hours on the telephone in order that they may gather a hundred people together in a large room where they will all fill the air with smoke and make a great deal of noise and roar at one another and clap their hands and stagger home at last patting one another on the back with the assurance that they have all done great things to spread the Kingdom of God.[16]

A spiritual home built on the frenetic pursuit of distracting irrelevancies may help a go-getter build an impressive resumé. But it also traps him on a treadmill that, for all its illusion of progress, goes nowhere. Such was the unhappy fate of J. F. Powers' clerical hustler Father Urban, who awoke one morning to find his curriculum vitae full and his soul empty.

Home as Labyrinth

Household deities are rusted gods, dismal fetishes. We genuflect before them out of a frightened need for the safety and power we think their approval brings. The strategy backfires, however, slamming us into prison cells of spiritual dullness, insipidity, oppressiveness, and irrelevance. Entropy may look good from the outside. But when all is said and done, the function of a fairy palace is to bewitch.

Still, as Mircea Eliade once pointed out, fetishes gesture, howsoever clumsily, at the wilderness God; embedded deeply within them is an intuition, murkily inarticulate and confused as it may be, of desert wind.[17] So it is with our four household gods. The problem is that they distort the truth by over-emphasizing a single aspect of the spiritual life to the exclusion of all others. Of course the head should be called into service in our search for God, but not at the sacrifice of the heart. Conversely, while "sweet consolations" certainly can play a role in our spiritual growth, they oughtn't to be taken as the one and only goal. Worshippers of the syllogistic and orgy-porgy gods forget these points.

Similarly, no one would deny that a healthy spirituality is grounded in obedience to divine will and a striving to do good. But this isn't at all the same as lockstep conformity to bewilderingly detailed coda or frenetic worldly bustling. Obedience must be complemented by autonomous risk-taking, and good works by a noble will. The lopsidedness of the codex and resumé gods upsets this balance.

Worship of household gods is skewed in a more general way as well. We've seen that followers of the syllogistic and orgy-porgy gods are subjectivists, dwelling exclusively in either the intellect or the emotions. Devotees of the codex and resumé gods err in the other direction: They downplay interiority by immersing themselves in external rules or good works. But just as an authentic spiritual life is a delicate balance of mind and emotion, obedience and freedom, and intention and act, so it's also a synthesis of the inner and the outer. When we focus too sharply on the interior, we lose touch with the world. When we spend ourselves externally, we forget our souls. Either alternative locks us into a deserted temple cluttered with dusty altars and broken-down gods. Our "native clay symbols," says the poet Jack Clemo, grow "unreal."[18]

Then we begin to gasp for air, crushed by what the sixteenth-century reformer John Calvin chillingly called "anxiety of the labyrinth." The Latin root of "anxiety" literally means the feeling of being constricted and suffocated. Fidelity to iron gods traps us inside a "terrible" labyrinth "of evils" whose closeness breeds a stifled sense of spiritual claustrophobia. The walls begin to move in; what we intended as havens become airless mazes that torment us

until we bang our fists against their walls in sheer despera-
tion.[19] As Rilke dryly remarks, we are no longer "at home in
our interpreted world."[20]

Calvin's labyrinth is a symbol of the spiritual alienation
we bring on ourselves when we succumb to the entropic
allure of household *lares*. Narcissus imprisons himself in lifeless abstractions; Bernard leaves the Solidarity Service with a
crushing sense of incompleteness; Nicodemus feels hemmed
in by his own elaborate legalisms; and Father Urban's mad-
cap scramble to build the Kingdom of God only distances
him from its gates.

The irony of it all would be laughable if it weren't so sad:
Home, the one place we should fit in, is desolately, forbid-
dingly, suffocatingly alien. Once the iron gods begin to rust,
once the fetishes start molting their feathers and shells, the
household altar is cause for anxiety rather than celebration.
It's at this point that the soul stands at the desert's edge, reeling between nostalgia for its lost home and horror at the fetid
labyrinth home has become. The situation seems hopeless.
The labyrinth has no exit.

Desert Wind, Desert Choice

When we allow our fears and insecurities to alienate us
from the desert God and trap us inside the labyrinth, no
struggle on our part, howsoever valiant, can succeed in free-
ing us. Every gesture of resistance only adds sinew to the
walls, because they draw their strength from obstinate self-
assertion. The will to hold back ambiguity, the will to tame
mystery, the will to manipulate iron-solid *lares*—willfulness
fashioned the very bricks and mortar that now imprison us.

So there's nothing we can do on our own steam to break
through. In spite of this, however, there *is* a way out: The

labyrinth can be toppled by the desert wind. But the divine sirocco will not liberate unless we acquiesce to it. To do that, we must heed the call of the desert God, the God who refuses to be fetishized by concepts, emotions, rules, or deeds.

The amazing thing is that we're programmed to hear the summons from the very moment of our conception. Our subsequent lapse into *lares* worship may dull the sensitivity of our receptors, but the receptors themselves are indestructible. The desert whence the wind blows isn't an actual place of sand and rock, but the still point within our hearts where God and the true self dwell. That place, as we'll see in chapter 5, is untouchable by entropy.

Karl Rahner refers to the call of the inner desert as divine grace, the hushed summons of the God of mystery. Grace whispers continuously, riding on every heartbeat, every breath we draw. It is "present irremovably," underlying each one of our experiences as a "prior apprehension of the all-transcending whole which is the mystery, one and nameless."[21] Our ironclad souls may suppress conscious awareness of this deep-down still point, but its echoes reverberate even through the slush of entropy.

So desert grace is always available. It may seem to us that the wind blows when it will, but this is a false impression. The desert wind ceaselessly gusts. That we experience it only sporadically comes from our unwillingness to open up to it, not from an ebb and flow in the wind itself.

But there are moments in our lives—"decisive moments," Rahner calls them—when the wind "breaks in upon our awareness...with irresistible force."[22] Following Ignatius of Loyola, Rahner argues that there are three such moments.[23] One is the sudden and undeniable summons, a lightning bolt that instantly hurls the hearer into the heart of divine mystery.

Another is the call of quiet infusion, when grace gently halts the self's noisy activity and wafts it toward the still point.

These two moments are rare. Very few of us awaken to the desert from either a Damascus road flash or a soft immersion in silent mystery. Spiritual suffocation is the third and more common decisive moment: Most ironclad souls only take notice of the wind of grace after their spiritual homes become labyrinthine prisons. When the "graspable contours of our everyday realities break and dissolve";[24] when the household gods that once proudly glittered begin to tarnish and peel; when bitter experience forces an acknowledgment that staying at home will smother and slay us; when we finally reach the point of despising our spiritual entropy: only then, in the midst of anguish and desolation, do most of us feel the wind blowing through our hair. Only then do we attend to the summons.

But hearing the call is one thing, following it another. There's no automatic liberation in the third decisive moment. Instead, a choice is demanded of us, what Kierkegaard called the great "Either/Or": *either* we allow the wind to carry us where it will—into the desert—*or* we stop our ears and perversely hunker down in our labyrinths. "Either/Or," says Kierkegaard, "is the key to heaven,"[25] but it's up to us to fit it in the lock.

Speaking of the necessity of an Either/Or choice here may seem to contradict the earlier observation that no act of the will can liberate us from the labyrinth of anxiety into which our household gods have driven us. A choice, after all, is an act of the will.

But there are choices and there are choices. Some are egoistic acts whose only aim is to steamroll over any obstacle that stands in the way of self-aggrandizement. These choices are forward thrusts in the ego's campaign to carve out a safe place for itself. But the choice demanded from us by the great

Either/Or is one of relinquishment rather than assertion, acquiescence rather than resistance, surrender rather than assault. When we make a choice *for* the desert, we suborn our will *to* the desert. We strip ourselves of the right of self-determination and ask the great wilderness mystery to take us. The choice demanded of us when we hear the summons, then, is paradoxical: It is the choice to cease choosing, the will to unwill. Either way, facing the great Either/Or is a crisis of terrific proportion.

It's terrifying, first, because it permits no compromise. When the wind of grace blows through us, it allows only two options: remain where we are or go into the wilderness. Hang onto the will or let it go. Cleave to domesticated gods or bare one's throat to the feral desert God. Either alternative is so frightening that many of us yearn for a third way out, one that liberates us from the labyrinth without shoving us into the wilderness. Instead of an Either/Or, we want a both-and that allows us to assert our "own will," as Kierkegaard says, but "in such a way that the name of God is brought into conjunction with it, whereby man thinks he is assured against being ungodly."[26]

No such option is available. The desert God will not accept a both-and, and to hold out for it is "alas, precisely...the most aggravated sort of ungodliness."[27] It's a desperate struggle of the self to assert its will, to cut a deal with God on its own terms. But the halfway measure of both-and won't do. The only way out of the labyrinth is surrender. As Kierkegaard ominously says, what the desert God demands

> is a total transformation in a man, to wrest from him through renunciation and self-denial all that, and precisely that, to which he immediately clings, in which he immediately has his life.[28]

The great Either/Or is terrifying in the second place because it permits no hesitation. When the decisive moment arrives, we must choose immediately. We don't have the luxury of careful scrutiny; we can't afford to take the time to make a checklist of pros and cons. The longer we hesitate to allow the wind to carry us into the desert, the greater the likelihood we'll never escape the labyrinth. Grace-filled opportunity must be embraced when it comes, not deposited in a spiritual vault for future withdrawal. *Time Jesum transeuntem et non revertentem:* "Dread the passage of Jesus, for he does not return." So hesitation isn't an option when summoned by the desert. Either we stay where we are, or we leap.

But the final terror of the great Either/Or is the most formidable one: the dreadful emptiness of the desert to which we're called.

Humans are basically conservative creatures. We resist change, especially radical change, even if we find the status quo barely tolerable. Hellish as it is, it's at least a hell we're familiar with. It may torment us, but it won't bewilder us with unexpected blows. But change propels us into the unknown, into an unmapped terrain whose darkness paralyzes us with foreboding. So we cling to the enemy we know in order to escape the one we don't.

When faced with the decisive moment of the Either/Or, we're called to make a change so radical that Kierkegaard calls it the "heaviest trial" imaginable.[29] The radical nature of the change is obvious: turning our backs on the only home we've known. But it's also the heaviest trial because we sense that the new land the desert wind is pushing us toward will be the death of us. We look into the empty wilderness and crumple with a nauseous, sweating panic. The panic of vertigo strikes. We suddenly feel as if we're perched atop a tall building, leaning into the perilous slope of its steep roof.

John Calvin called this roofwalking dread the "abyss of misery," and saw it as the counterpoint to labyrinth anxiety. If the one crushes us with spiritual claustrophobia, the other sickens us with spiritual agoraphobia. When we suffer from labyrinth anxiety, the walls close in. But with the abyss of misery, the absence of boundaries torments us. Anxiety born of the oppressive sense of too much gives way to anxiety caused by a sense of absolutely nothing.

Looking into the abyss of misery, we feel as if we're in danger of being flung into a sinister pit of formless chaos and bottomless confusion. We know, even if we dare not admit, that the abyss is a void that will dissolve the self into a great nothingness, a chaos lacking, according to Calvin, "form or semblance or anything whatsoever."[30] To balance on the roof is to know the horror of the unlimited.

The twentieth-century author Peter Bowles perfectly captures the uncanny dread that overwhelms us when we confront desert emptiness. In a scene from his novel *The Sheltering Sky*, the two main characters, Port and Kit, sit on a rock in the Sahara Desert and gaze at the horizon. Port speaks.

> "You know, the sky here's very strange. I often have the sensation when I look at it that it's a solid thing up there, protecting us from what's behind."
> Kit shuddered slightly as she said: "From what's behind?"
> "Yes."
> "But what *is* behind?" Her voice was very small.
> "Nothing, I suppose. Just darkness. Absolute night."[31]

Port experiences the vertigo of Calvin's abyss when he feels the "darkness" and "absolute night" of the desert. The sky canopy that normally holds back the sheer nothingness we so dread is absent there. No household gods of iron can guard us in its wasteland, no *lares*-cocoons provide the illusion of solidity and security. When we step into the wilderness, we drop our weapons and tools and dive headfirst into a pitch blackness no eye can penetrate.

Given this, many of us—too many of us—freeze with indecision and remain suspended between the Either and the Or for the rest of our days. Merton expresses our dilemma well:

> The prospect of...wilderness is something that so appalls most people that they refuse to enter upon its burning sands and travel among its rocks. They cannot believe that contemplation and sanctity are to be found in a desolation where there is no food and no shelter and no refreshment for their imagination and intellect and the desires of their nature.[32]

So we hang in the balance, oppressed by our home and terrified of the wilderness alternative. We are like the man in the ancient parable who clings for dear life to a root jutting out of a sheer cliff wall. Above him, on the cliff ledge, awaits a loathsome serpent. If the man climbs back up, he will suffocate in its coils. Below him lies a fathomless chasm. If he releases his hold on the root, he will hurtle into its blank nothingness and die. So the hapless man simply tightens his grip and dangles, caught between the labyrinth and the abyss. With John of the Cross, he feels that "This life I live is no life at all":

> I no longer live within myself
> and I cannot live without God,

for having neither him nor myself
what will life be?
It will be a thousand deaths,
longing for my true life
and dying because I do not die.[33]

Heavy trials demand great courage, and only heroes are intrepid enough to heed the desert's summons and embark on the great adventure. But we need not cling to a life that is no life at all, because each of us carries the potential for heroism, each of us is capable of the great Either/Or decision to drop from the cliff wall into the abyss. And the very instant that choice is made, the doorless maze into which our worship of household gods drove us collapses—not because we've resisted, but because we've finally let go. The desert wind crashes through the labyrinth we were unable to escape on our own. Altar veils rip asunder, rusted gods wobble, and the walls of our temple sway and crash. When the dust settles and we look around us, blinking and disoriented, we find ourselves in the desert. The adventure begins in earnest.

Chapter Four

Desert Dying

Death Koan

The spiritual hero says "yes" to the great Either/Or and falls into the empty desert with the forlorn hope that her journey, dreadful as it is, is preferable to the labyrinth. But from the very beginning there's something wildly absurd about the whole undertaking. The home she left was an iron god who could protect but not-protect her, a god she could manipulate but not-manipulate. Her sanctuary was a prison she both yearned for and loathed. To break free of the prison she had to willingly unwill. The only refuge from labyrinth-suffocation available to her was abyss-dread. Paradox and contradiction surround her, koan tumbles on koan. And now that she's actually in the wilderness, now that she's embarked on the second stage of the journey, she trips across yet another koan, a terrifying koan: The life she seeks is death.

Make no mistake about it: The desert slays. Anyone foolish or desperate enough to go into the desert leaves her bones there. Whoever ventures into the koanic wilderness, as R. S. Thomas reminds us, knows her terrible fate:

> I have this that I must do
> One day: overdraw on my balance
> Of air, and breaking the surface
> ...go down into the...
> Darkness to search for the door
> To myself in dumbness and blindness
> And uproar of scared blood
> At the eardrums.[1]

Christianity is koanic through and through, and so is the language of Jesus, the supreme Koan, the Koan incarnate. He's a great riddler, partly because he's a mischievous teaser, but mainly because what he wants to get across can only be said in the absurd language of paradox. And one of the most bewildering koans he throws at us is the incomprehensibility that we must die when we enter the life-giving desert. The weight Jesus gives this death koan is suggested by the fact that it's the opening beatitude in his Sermon on the Mount, which in turn is scripture's most comprehensive statement on the spiritual life. The beatitude is usually translated into English as "Blessed are the poor in spirit, for theirs is the kingdom of heaven" (Matt 5:3). Everything else Jesus said in the sermon—and, indeed, everything he taught throughout his entire public ministry—is a gloss on this riddle.

The first beatitude's uncanniness comes through even in translation: In order to be richly happy, one must be poor. But its utter weirdness is especially striking in the Greek.

In the first place, the phrase "blessed are," which prefaces this and each one of the other nine beatitudes, is curious. It's a rendering of *makarios,* a word that suggests a state of unruffled bliss, joy, and prosperity. When an individual attains *makarios,* she experiences a godlike contentment. She lacks nothing, nor can her *makarios* be disrupted by anything. She is genuinely happy and fulfilled.

In the second place, the "poor" in the phrase "poor in spirit" is equally perplexing. There are two words in Greek that English renders as "poor"—*penes* and *ptoches*—but their meanings are quite different. *Penes* refers to the condition of a person who endlessly drudges to eke out a bare, marginal existence. Slaves and unskilled laborers live in a state of *penes.* There is no superfluity in their lives, no rainy day resources to fall back on when misfortune strikes. They toil each day for the day's scanty bread, and arise the next morning to do the same thing all over again.

But *penes*-poverty, brutal as it is, is nothing compared to *ptoches*-poverty. The poor person who toils to survive may have nothing to spare, but at least she squeaks by. The person in a state of *ptoches,* on the other hand, is hopelessly destitute, starving, beggarly. Everything has been taken from her, and she finds herself on the streets, abjectly dispossessed of life's essentials, sunk in miserable squalor and utterly dependent on whatever bits of food strangers toss her way. The horror of *ptoches* is emphasized by its root, *ptossein,* a verb meaning "to cower or crouch." Persons who are *ptoches* have fallen over the margin of survival and cower in absolute deprivation. Their life is a curse.

It would've been strange enough had Jesus used the word *penes* in the first beatitude: "Joyful and fulfilled and prosperous are those who are so poor that they live precariously on the margin." Even those tempted to romanticize poverty would find such a bizarre claim offensive. But koan-master that he is, Jesus has no use for halfway measures. So he pushes us headfirst into absurdity by using *ptoches* instead of *penes:* "Joyful and fulfilled and prosperous are those so completely destitute that they cower in hopeless misery." *Blessed are those who are cursed:* With this dark beatitude, Jesus doesn't merely assault reason; he chills the heart as well.

Nor does the savagery of the koan end here. Jesus goes on to make sure his listeners know he's talking about spiritual, not material, destitution: *ptochoi tou pneumati,* "poor in spirit." To be deprived of the minimal essentials for physical survival is horrible. But to be stripped naked of interior possessions is unspeakable. Perhaps it's possible—although just barely—to lose job, property, reputation, even loved ones, and still hold onto a modicum of inner equilibrium. But even this is taken away when we fall into spiritual *ptoches.* Hope, faith, trust, confidence, intellect, imagination, feelings, one's very sense of personal identity: when we lose these, we've sunk as low as it gets. This, surely, is the death of us. Yet Jesus proclaims (and one must imagine him doing so with twinkling eyes and laughing voice) that this death is a great blessing, a wondrous prosperity, a state of fulfillment, an entry into life abundant.

When we drop from the cliff-wall of the great Either/Or, we fall into the abyss of soul wilderness. And what awaits us in the darkness at the bottom is the death koan Jesus unleashed in the Sermon on the Mount.

Demons

We can never fully grasp the death koan. Koans hold truth, but a truth that must be lived rather than seized and uttered. The death koan forever lies on the other side of reason.

But even though a koan is beyond rational comprehension—or perhaps *because* it is—its mystery catalyzes awareness of what hovers around the edge of its unsayable core. When we embrace a koan, it radiates a dark light that gradually illumines hitherto unnoticed aspects of existence. Staring directly into a koan blinds us. But if we take the koan as a reference point and direct our gaze to one side or the other of it, we discover that our peripheral vision is strangely sharpened. What once was dim and foggy comes into focus.

So it is with the death koan. If we try a frontal assault, it slips out of our range. But if we stand back and look sideways, the incomprehensibility of its "death is life" claim sheds light on who we are and where we're going in the desert.

The death koan's first ray of illumination spotlights the demons who possess us. When we undertake the journey toward the death which is life, we are beset by the imps of the wilderness.

Desert sojourners have known and written about these imps—the same ones who inhabit Hopkins' mountains of the mind—for hundreds of years. In the first centuries of Christianity, the men and women who fled into the desert to live as religious hermits encountered them crouching under every rock and lurking in every crevice. Their struggles with the demons became a favorite theme of religious folklore. Who among us today doesn't know of the terrific battle St. Anthony fought with the legion of desert demons? And

Anthony is just the most familiar example; each of the desert hermits waged his or her own private war.

Medieval artists were particularly fascinated by stories of wilderness demons. In transferring these tales onto canvas, they usually depicted the imps as hideous night prowlers with gaping jaws, razor-sharp talons, multiple limbs, leering eyes. But what terrifies one age strikes another as silly. We twentieth-century sophisticates are more tickled than terrified by the illustrations in medieval books on demonology. To our eyes, there's something rather goofy about the bizarre creatures spun from the medieval imagination. They strike us as clownish.

But we ought not mock. The demons are real. True, they aren't physical entities who actually inhabit exterior deserts. But they still exist. They're our own spawn, coughed up from the pit of the private hell bubbling within each of us. As Karl Rahner says, there is a subterranean darkness in us

> to which, although [it] may be part of us, we have no easy access, [a] depth in which demons may well lurk. It is full of mysterious psychic realities behind each of which stands something even more concealed and incomprehensible....There is within us a confusion of drives and possibilities....[2]

When we go into soul wilderness, the psychic demons burst through the gates of our inner inferno and fly out to gibber and spit and slash.

In the sixteenth century, the philosopher René Descartes proposed a radically dualistic account of human nature. He argued that each person is a patchwork of two independent and irreducible substances: mind and body, "thinking" and "extended" substance. The specifics of Descartes' dualism don't work for a number of reasons (not the least of which is his failure to explain how mind and body interact), but his general intuition was correct. Humans *are* dualistic creatures, composed not of two irreducible substances but of two selves. One is the true self, who we really are. The other is a false self, an illusion we take for reality: the pretender self.

The true self (which we'll explore more fully in the next chapter) was described by the fourteenth-century mystic Meister Eckhart as the "core of the soul...sensitive to nothing but the divine Being, unmediated. Here God enters the soul with all he has and not in part. He enters the soul through its core and nothing may touch that core except God himself."[3] This soul-core, which Eckhart says is found in saint and sinner alike,[4] is the source of the "prior apprehension" of God Karl Rahner speaks about. The core links us to God because the core contains God; and because God is supremely real, the core is that within us which is most real, the center of gravity which sustains the orbit of our being. It is our true self. But like the God whence it comes and which it contains, the true self is clouded in mystery, darkly and silently unknowable, neither conscious nor subconscious, but supraconscious.[5] It can be experienced but not thought. It is a koan.

By contrast, the false or pretender self is the ego: that artificial "me" we fancy both constitutes our real identity and regulates the buzz of psychological activity that goes on within us at the conscious and unconscious levels. The combination of that activity—ideas, images, emotions, fears and insecurities, appetites, conflicts, ingrained habits, and cultural internalizations—plus the "me," which is somehow majestically in control of the psychic buzz, we typically refer to as "personality." This "me," the switchboard operator in the center of personality, is what we think of when we think of the self. For most of us, says Merton, there is "no greater subjective reality" than the "me," and it quickly becomes "the fundamental reality of life to which everything else in the universe is ordered."[6]

But the "me" is a pretender self. It only plays at being who we really are, and its claim to sovereignty is mere conceit: Far from coordinating and controlling the psychic switchboard, the "me" in fact is at its beck and call. Even worse, the "me" takes its own delusion of authority so seriously that it ignores the silent echoes of Eckhart's core, the true self. Thus the "me" confuses its own pretensions to selfhood with actual selfhood, and the upshot, in Merton's words, is that "the deep secrecy of my being is often hidden from me by my own estimate of what I am."[7]

So long as we dwell comfortably at home, we remain bamboozled by the pretensions of the pretender self, confident that we know who we are and that we control our inner drives. Granted, there may be occasional instances of doubt or uneasiness, interludes when a panicked suspicion flashes through us that things are out of hand. These moments of "me"-doubt are generally discounted as nervous head colds, however, best treated by the latest self-esteem therapy.

But when a spiritual crisis hits, such as the "decisive moment" of discovering that our homes are actually suffocating labyrinths, the pretender self can't rise to the occasion. Piecemealed as it is from illusion and conceit, it falls to pieces if it runs up against a genuine challenge. So when the "me" tumbles into the great emptiness of the desert, when it can no longer hide behind the false gods who fed its delusions of power and security, it finally sees itself for the paltry insubstantiality it is. There are no protective screens in the desert, nowhere to hide. In the desert we are utterly isolated for the first time in our life—plunged "Into the night, on and on/The lamps fade; and the stars. We are alone"[8]—and that alone-ness forces us to fix our gaze on our inner hell. The false light through which we hitherto viewed ourselves winks out, and in the pitiless darkness the false self, stripped of its pretensions of control and self-sufficiency, desolately realizes

> I am not myself, it suddenly appears,
> but horrible habits, habits, habits....[9]

This is the sickening moment when the desert demons, the neurotic fears and insecurities, the vainglorious ambitions and tarnished loves and shameful drives, roar out from their psychic pit to gambol in the dark and wail their banshee song. They jab and prod and poke us, scornfully laughing at our shattered pretensions, mocking our smarmy conceit. *You sap!* they howl. *You thought you controlled us, when all along it was we who puppet-stringed you!* In their grotesque gyrations we see the corruption and lie our life has been, and we fall quaking to the ground.

First Death

The Hasidic sage Menahem Mendl of Kotzk once stunned his followers with words of darkest night. He was preaching on the Genesis verse that says everything was *tohu-bohu*, formless and void, before the primordial act of creation. Then, in the middle of his sermon, he threw the bombshell: What Genesis doesn't dare reveal is that everything is *still* formless and void. Everywhere, nothing but *tohu-bohu*.[10]

The Kotzker's claim is absurd if we assume, as his startled disciples did, that he was referring to the physical order. It, obviously, is neither formless nor void. But if we move from outer to inner terrain, the Kotzker's assertion begins to make sense. The desert's assault upon the "me" plunges us into a chaotic world of *tohu-bohu* where the needle on our compass twirls madly.

After the initial shock of discovering the lie we are, after the "me" to which we've pinned our identity breaks apart like dozens of crows flying in different directions, the stricken desert wanderer generally tries to rally. She's an old hand at self-deception and rationalization, and now she musters all her skills of legerdemain to convince herself that the darkness into which she's fallen is just another episode of garden variety nerves. So she defies the darkness, just as she's scorned all foes in the past, and struggles to regain her throne.

Okay, she tells herself. *Maybe I'm not the all-together person I always thought I was. Maybe there are dark spots within me I need to work on. But I can still fix things. I'm still in control!* Armed with this whistling-against-the-dark courage, she again and again tries to recapture the crow-imps of the splintered ego, to throw a net over them and show them who's boss. All she needs is self-discipline, determination, resolve. But the crows are too crafty for such tricks. They see right through them. Once released by the solitude of the desert, they can't be tamed again (as if they ever really could). They jeer at the "me's" efforts to hang on to the illusion of control. Perched safely atop the ruins of rusted gods, they laugh at the increasingly desperate efforts of the "me" to re-establish itself.

When the bone-weary pretender self at last collapses to the ground in despair; when it feels the biting sand against its cheek and admits once and for all that the sovereign "me" is a myth, that in fact the "me" is nothing but a vile Pandora's box of uncontrollable imps; when it looks in fear and shame and hatred and rage at what it really is rather than what it imagined itself to be: when this bitter moment arrives, the last pretensions of "me"-hood slip through our fingers and we fall into the Kotzker's *tohu-bohu*.

This is the first death awaiting us in the desert.

In thinking about death, what typically comes to mind is the ceasing-to-be of the physical body. But the body's dissolution isn't what fundamentally defines death for most of us. Fearful as biological death is, we dread even more the ceasing-to-be of our personal identity. We can endure the loss of a limb or an eye, we can bear up under the burden of illness and physical debilitation, if only we feel assured that the "me" will abide—that regardless of how ravaged the body becomes, our personal identity will still flicker. Physical death frightens us, but the prospect of losing our sense of self, the "me"-center of gravity that infuses meaning into our existence, sends us scampering in horror. If that goes, everything goes. As a character in one of Albert Camus' plays says, "To lose one's life is a little thing....But to see the sense of this life dissipated, to see our reason for existence disappear: this is what is insupportable."[11]

Yet personal identity is precisely what we lose in the first desert death. Our point of reference evaporates, the battery that generated direction and purposefulness runs dry, and *tohu-bohu* engulfs us. John of the Cross calls this unspeakably bleak moment when the desert strips away our sense of identity the "dark night of the senses."[12] We stand utterly alone in the darkness and helplessly watch as everything that once defined who we are is revealed for the demonic whirlpool it is. And when the pretender self's last illusion evaporates, what's left over—a limp bundle of dry skin and bones pecked at by nether world crows—crumples to the ground and dies.

But the desert is mercilessly thorough. It's not finished with us yet. For the death we've died in losing the pretender self is only a preliminary destruction, a first death. We've been impoverished by the loss of our identities, but the impoverishment is one of *penes* rather than *ptoches*. *Tohu-bohu* has swallowed up our sense of "me," our internal compass. But we're still not utterly destitute. We haven't fallen as far as we can and must. The bones and skin remain.

Not for long.

Second Death

The poet Wallace Stevens, himself no stranger to the desert, once wrote that when a person descends into the chaos of *tohu-bohu* and no longer has "a belief on which to rely," there still remains "the fundamental animal."[13] Stevens's meaning is cryptic, but most likely what he wants to evoke with "the fundamental animal" allusion is that gut urge for survival, that inarticulate hope of somehow hanging on, that still glows feebly in a person who's lost his identity and self-direction to the first death.

One is reminded here of the insight Victor Frankl arrived at during his internment in a Nazi death camp. Frankl's bitter experience was that the entire camp apparatus was designed to break those inmates who survived the initial "selection" by reducing them to gray-faced automatons stripped of any sense of self. The prisoners who had the best chance of survival, observed Frankl, were those who managed to cling, howsoever tenuously, to *hope*—hope in a future less horrific than the present.[14] Frankl's "hope" is Stevens's "fundamental animal," and it's all that stirs in the parched bag of skin and bones left by the first death.

But hope in what? That God will rescue us from our *penes*-poverty, from the *tohu-bohu* of shattered identity, from the forlornness of the dark night. After the first death, we acknowledge our helplessness. We no longer pretend we're in control; we don't even know who we are anymore, nor where we are. We are lost. But deep within us, so deep that it barely breaks surface, is a final shred of hope that the mysterious God of the desert will pity us and take away the cup of wormwood. How could he not? Fierce and formidable as he is, God also loves. If we wait patiently, he will come.

What little remains of us latches onto this hope as a drowning person seizes a bit of flotsam. Supplications, with withered arms and reddened eyes and parched throat, rise from the desert floor. *I'm in your hands. I can do nothing on my own. Help me!* cries the pitiful thing we've become. With our face in the sand, we listen for a response.

The hope that sustained the inmates Frankl writes about was appropriate and good in the concentration camps, but it's just another obstacle in the desert. There, even the humblest yearning for God, the faintest fundamental-animal hope, which is all that's left us in our *penes,* stands in the way. Hope is a form of passive resistance, a subtle defiance of the present for the sake of the future. But resistance, even the passive kind, even resistance that rides on abject humility, is a stirring of the will. It's a nay-saying that refuses *tohu-bohu,* a last-ditch effort to cling to the edge of the chasm, a struggle to maintain some degree, minimal as it is, of autonomy. As such, the hope for God is a self-serving rebellion that forestalls the advent of the desert God.

So the response we await never comes. Nothing breaks the silence of *tohu-bohu.* Scorching days and frigid nights flow into weeks, and then months, and God remains silent. Hope grows brittle and gives way first to bewilderment and then an enraged sense of betrayal. Hands once raised in supplication now curl into angry fists shaken at an empty sky. *Why have you led me into the desert to die? Why have you forsaken me? Are my pleas nothing more than water poured into the sand?* Silence. Everywhere there is only aloneness and absence and abandonment. Then the fundamental animal perishes; the implacable God of the desert takes even that away from us. And when hope departs, we slip over the margin of *penes* into *ptoches*. Utterly destitute, completely stripped, unspeakably beggared, we implode in the vacuum John of the Cross calls the "dark night of the spirit."[15] Bones and hide fall to dust and the dust is scattered by the unforgiving desert sirocco. Nothing remains. We are voided and formless. We are *tohu-bohu.*

This is the second death.

Decreation

In her posthumously published notes on the mystical way, Simone Weil distinguishes between "destruction" and "decreation." Her reflections shed light on the *ptoches* of the second death.

Destruction, says Weil, "make[s] something created pass into nothingness," whereas decreation "make[s] something created pass into the uncreated." Decreation leads us to the desert God; destruction is a "blameworthy substitute."[16] Obviously the key to the distinction Weil wants to make lies in what she means by "nothingness" and "the uncreated."

As we'll discover in the next chapter, the word "nothingness" has frequently been used by spiritual authors to evoke the mystery of God: Whatever God is, God is no-thing. But Weil doesn't intend this meaning here. For her, "nothingness" connotes a wasteland state of alienation from the divine Source of existence. Nothingness is that condition of God-deprivation the pretender self abides in so long as it clings to the conviction that it is real. An illusion, after all, is a nothing. It has less substance than a flickering shadow, and to embrace an illusion about the self and about God is to sink into an exilic limbo located on the far side of the universe. Our being comes from and is sustained by divine Being, and when our willfulness denies the dependency, we blameworthily self-destruct into alienated nothingness.

Uncreatedness, on the other hand, is the unencumbered innocence achieved when the two desert deaths purge us of the willfulness by which we've separated ourselves from God and "sift" us, as Denise Levertov says, "between thoughtful fingers" into "finer substance."[17] Decreation is a return to the starting line, as it were, to a spiritual state before the pretender self's demonic fears and insecurities and hubris seduced it to the altar of household gods. When we decreate, all that stands between us and God—including our very yearning for God—is blanked out, restoring the pure potentiality we were before our waywardness created the corrupt "me" we became. What remains is an unblemished capacity to enter into God, an unmitigated openness to the mystery of the desert. What remains, as the Buddhists say, is our "original face."

Weil's discussion reminds us of a great irony in the spiritual life. When we feel most secure, powerful, confident, and self-sufficient, we are nothing. We are most abjectly *not*. But when we're stripped naked by desert despair, helplessly and hopelessly decreated of all our facades and deceptions, we are most real, most substantial. We *are*. Our being is proportionate to the destitution forced on us by the wilderness. "There are," says Weil, "only two instants of perfect nudity and purity in human life: birth and death,"[18] with "nudity" and "purity" here meaning an unsullied openness to God. When we die the second desert death, these two instants become one.

Back in the sixteenth century, Catherine of Genoa anticipated the spirit if not the vocabulary of Weil's distinction between destruction and decreation. Catherine realized that the pretender self is destructively "alienated from all spiritual things that could give it solace and joy." But when the soul lands in the purgatorial desert, the painful process of dealienation begins. In the desert, the self progressively loses its destructive attachment to

> the things of the intellect, will, or memory,
> and in no manner tends more to one thing
> than to another.
> Quite still and in a state of siege,
> the me within finds itself gradually stripped
> of all those things that in spiritual or bodily form
> gave it some comfort.

When the last alienating illusion of hope is decreated and the old self is completely destitute, Catherine promises that the desert death brings "final consummation," "full actualization."[19]

Weil and Catherine, as well as many other chroniclers of the desert journey, remind us that decreation is frightfully agonizing—not because the God of the desert enjoys inflicting pain, or even because there's intrinsic value in suffering, but because the pretender self's alienation is so engrained. Entrenched habits are stubborn, addictions recalcitrant. Once a foothold is established, they grow cement-hard. Purgative death in the desert is violent because nothing less can crack the casing of a soul enmired in entropy.

Vanishing Point

In the private notebook where she scribbled her thoughts on purgative decreation, Simone Weil includes a brief passage that gets to the mystical heart of what it means to die in the desert. Decreation, she writes, is an "imitation of God's renunciation in creation. In a sense, God renounces being everything. We should renounce being something. That is our only good."[20] These words are reminiscent of the profoundly important kabbalistic notion of *tsimtsum* taught by one of the greatest of Jewish mystics, the sixteenth-century Isaac ben Solomon Luria.

Luria's doctrine of *tsimtsum* has been too ignored by spiritual authors. It's unlikely that Weil herself knew of it. Although she was born into a Jewish household, her parents were thoroughly secularized; moreover, Weil's own adult antipathy to Judaism and the Hebrew religious tradition bordered, sadly, on bigotry. Nonetheless, traditional desert asceticism as well as Weil's thoughts on decreative renunciation are incredibly enriched when read in the light of *tsimtsum*.

Luria's starting point is the ancient Midrashic teaching that the Shekhinah, God's divine presence and power, is contracted into a single point within the holy of holies, the tabernacle. Intrigued by this suggestion of divine "constriction" or *tsimtsum*, Luria adapted it in order to make sense of the original act of cosmic creation.

Divine Being, said Luria, is infinite and eternal, all in all. But if this had always been the case, nothing ought now to be but God. Clearly, however, this isn't true: the world and its inhabitants—that is, things *not* God—are. So, Luria concluded, the coming-to-be of the universe must have been preceded by a voluntary withdrawal of God into himself to "make room," as it were, for created things. In shrinking into himself, in renouncing absolute plenitude, God allowed a primordial space, a sheer nothing, from which the created order could emerge. First withdrawal, then outpouring—this was the sequence of how the world came to be. The contemporary scholar of Jewish mysticism Gershom Scholem summarizes Luria's *tsimtsum* this way:

> The first act of...the Infinite Being is therefore not a step outside but a step inside, a movement of recoil, of falling back upon oneself, of withdrawing into oneself. Instead of emanation we have the opposite, contraction. The God who revealed himself in firm contours was superseded by one who descended deeper into the recesses of His own Being, who concentrated Himself into Himself, and had done so from the very beginning of the creation.[21]

Luria's doctrine of *tsimtsum* strikingly complements the Christian conviction that divine love is sacrificial by implying that the Incarnation's self-emptying was prefigured by a primordial self-emptying. The latter paved the way for original creation, the former for spiritual re-creation. Moreover, God's self-withdrawal in both creative acts suggests that constriction is the template for the soul's journey toward spiritual rebirth. First the contraction of decreation, of desert death, then the creative expansion into God.

This ebb-in-order-to-flow is what Weil has in mind when she says we must renounce being something just as God renounced being everything. When we enter the desert, we step out of the external world and dive deeply into the interior one: an initial contraction. We endure the shrinkage and disappearance of the ego in the first death and the vanishment of hope in the second: more contraction. We slim down progressively, withdrawing from everything we once were, becoming a decreation for the sake of re-creation. We face non-being in order to be. Thus the hero's journey into the wilderness—leaving home, leaving self, leaving the hope for God—is a replay of the creation mystery.

Yet human constriction is only analogous to God's constriction. The two differ in a couple of significant ways. First, God's voluntary shrinkage is undertaken for the sake of humans. God "gets out of the way" so that creation has breathing space to flourish. But when we undergo purgation in the wilderness, the soul—or, more precisely, the "me," the imp-infested pretender self—"gets out of the way" to make room for God. Everything that roadblocks God's coming, everything that alienates us from Being and hence hinders its unconcealment in the empty desert, contracts. The "me" decreatively recedes until it reaches the vanishing point of death. Only then is there room for God.

Second, while divine *tsimtsum* is self-initiated, human *tsimtsum* almost never is. A handful of people in each generation are so attuned to their preconceptual awareness of the desert God that they willingly step into the purgative furnace to char away what flakes of entropy still cling to them. Yet the truth of the matter is that these sensitive souls are few and far between. The rest of us burrow deeply into our household temples to cultivate the pretender self. We may admire—from a safe distance—mystical language about dying to make room for God, but what we really think is that only a lunatic would voluntarily renounce a comfortable spirituality for a wilderness journey of pain and death. Who voluntarily embraces *ptoches?* Who agrees to the erosion of personal identity? Who willingly endures not just the loss of sham entropic gods but also of God himself? Who wants to die?

Both Weil and Catherine astutely recognize that the impetus for human *tsimtsum* typically must originate outside human will in grace—the grace of the decisive moment, the grace of the two deaths. Weil admits that she needs God "to take her by force." Otherwise, the perilous nature of the desert adventure would send her reeling in horror.[22] Catherine observes that the soul "does not leave its prison or seek to do so until God has done all that is necessary" to push it out of home and into the uncharted wilderness.[23] True, the person whose iron gods have rusted is called to make a choice when confronted by the great Either/Or. But the choice is more response than initiative. The holy sirocco dust-coats household altars, turns dwelling places into prisons, and backs the homebody into a corner: either suffocate in the labyrinth or hurtle into the abyss. Stay where you are or enter the desert and die: Respond as you wish. This is bitter medicine, but nothing less extreme moves the timid self down the decreative path of *tsimtsum* toward eventual re-creation.

Saying "yes" to the great Either/Or, then, is really an assent to grim necessity. We leave home because the alternative is too bleak to contemplate. There's no joy in the assent, no high-spirited thrill of adventure, but only a scared recognition that since we can't stay where we are, we must acquiesce to banishment—and hope, as Catherine of Genoa hoped, for a "speedy death."[24]

A Wordless Page

There are many winds that blow from east to west, south to north. The exotic names of some are known: *aajej, ghibli, harmattan.* Others have no name, or their names go unspoken.

Some scorch, some freeze; some raise dust clouds, others pelt the earth with snow and ice. All are mysterious.[25]

But the most mysterious of all winds is the one called *tohu-bohu*. It is the wind out of the desert, and from its void all other winds are spawned. When it gusts through us we disintegrate in the vanishing point of *tsimtsum*. And *tsimtsum* is *ptoches*.

Nowhere is the mystery of the desert wind better evoked than by the British author Jim Crace. His novel *Quarantine* is a haunting chronicle of the wilderness fast of Jesus, whom Crace portrays as a touchingly naive, starry-eyed youth in quest of the Divine.

Jesus takes to the wilderness expecting he will be cleansed. But like all wilderness adventurers, he has no idea just how merciless the scouring will be. He thinks his desert quarantine will help him shed the impediments that stand between his soul and God's face. What he doesn't know is that *he* is the impediment.

But the desert knows, and quickly goes about instructing Jesus. A month of fasting melts away the youth's flesh and health, then his identity, and finally the very longing for God that drove him to the wasteland in the first place. By the end of his ordeal, Jesus' naive idealism has been supplanted first by pain, bewilderment, and despair, then by blank numbness. Shrunk in body and spirit and mind, he's at the evaporation point of *tsimtsum*. The furiously purgative wind of *tohu-bohu* has so emptied him of himself that

> he could not separate the wind from all the rushing in his ears. He was as numb as wood. They could have driven nails into his feet. He'd not have felt a thing.... His heart had decomposed. "Make sacrifices to god,

and then prepare yourself for the winds of judgement,"
the scriptures warned....He was the sacrifice.[26]

And then the moment of absolute disappearance into the
great *tohu-bohu* arrives. On the last morning of his fast, as
he fitfully dozes in the cave where he's taken shelter from
night beasts, Jesus hears a mighty, rushing wind. "He knew
what wind this was. This was the wind on which to fly away.
Its gusts and blusters came looking for him....Get up, get up,
it's time to go."[27] With his last strength Jesus crawls out of his
cave and painfully makes his way to a precipice that over-
looks the empty desert. "Naked to the wind," he opens his
arms to the void.

> The wind nudged round him, searching for a hold. He
> lifted slightly, felt his body parting from the rock. The
> earth had lost its pull on him. He was all surface, no
> inside. His leaf had fallen finally. He was a dry, dis-
> carded page of scripture now. The wind embraced him,
> rubbed the words off him. It made him blank. It made
> him ghostlier than air.
>
> ...Jesus was a voyager, at last, between the heavens and
> the earth. There was a light, deep in the middle of the
> night. He tried to swim to it. He tried to fly. He held his
> hands up to the light. His hands were bluey-white like
> glass. The light passed through. The mountain shivered
> from afar. He felt the cold of nothing there. He heard the
> cold of no one there. No god, no gardens, just the wind.[28]

This is *ptoches*.

Chapter Five

Divine Naught

All true ascesis as a desert lies:
hot wind, hot sand, no water, and no way.
The ego agonizes through each day.
Freedom is when it dies.

Jessica Powers

Fecund Chaos

Still, how can *ptoches* be *makarios?* Given the horror of desert death, the question seems even more baffling. Can dry bones live? The fatal plunge into *tohu-bohu, tsimtsum's* dissolution of not just our identity but also our life-line hope for God, chills the heart. Yet Jesus the riddler proclaims this destitution a blessed occasion.

Dov Baer, the great Hasidic maggid of Mezritch, suggests a way to enter more deeply into the death koan's mystery. Here's what he says.

> Nothing in the world can change from one reality into another, unless it first turns into nothing, that is, into the reality of the between-stage. In that stage it is nothing and no one can grasp it, for it has reached the rung

of nothingness, just as before creation. And then it is made into a new creature, from the egg to the chick. The moment when the egg is no more and the chick is not yet, is nothingness. And philosophy terms this the primal state which no one can grasp because it is a force which precedes creation; it is called chaos.[1]

What the maggid offers is a middle term that links *ptoches* with *makarios*. The *tohu-bohu* into which the wayfarer falls when she crosses the threshold of soul wilderness, that formless chaos that strips her down to the point of extinction, to the "rung of nothingness," is a gestation period, a "between-stage" separating what she once was from what she can become. Before bowing to the great Either/Or, she was a self-confident and spiritually comfortable homebody. That ends when the desert takes everything from her. Up close, such destitution strikes us as a curse. But from a more distant vantage point, it unconceals as an opportunity for decreatively slashing and burning away the demon-haunted forest of the pretender self so that the true self might emerge.

The anonymous author of the medieval *Cloud of Unknowing* makes a similar point. Soul wilderness horrifies us, he (or she) says, because it threatens our ego, that "greedy greyhound" whose only wish is to laze about and eat. As the desert wind blows in and through him, the greyhound grows disoriented, confused, and finally numb. His sleek complacency erodes and his gluttonous appetites quieten *(tsimtsum)* until he falls into a radical "forgetfulness" *(tohu-bohu).*[2] Like Crace's Jesus, he becomes a wordless page, a blankness that leaves room for a new text. From the perspective of the pretender self, this death-like erasure is horrifying: the *ptoches* of losing one's identity. But in fact it's a great blessing, because it's an opportunity for unimpeded flight. As the poet Hart Crane notes,

> Forgetfulness is like a bird whose wings are reconciled,
> Outspread and motionless—
> A bird that coasts the wind unwearyingly.[3]

The void of desert death, then, is the womb of decreative re-creation. It vacates the old self so that a fresh start can be made, and this means that the *ptoches* of radical forgetfulness is a painful but necessary alembic for the *makarios* of spiritual purification and awakening. Our "long sickness of health and living now begins to mend," and "nothing" brings us "all things."[4] Or as Meister Eckhart puts it, "The soul grows by subtraction rather than addition....If God is to come in, the creature must get out."[5]

Fusion

The Zen tradition teaches that forgetfulness leads to rebirth. As the disciple sinks ever deeper into her koan, self-consciousness and personal identity diminish until eventually nothing remains but formless void. Only then, when there's no longer a "me" separating koan and disciple, can enlightenment occur. This is what happens in *tohu-bohu*. The wayfarer sinks into soul wilderness, he disappears in the formless, voided sand, and from this between-stage of self-forgetfulness—the "still point," as Dame Julian of Norwich calls it[6]— arises the possibility of meeting God.

Julian's "still point" is what Eckhart refers to as "potential sensitivity,"[7] a phrase that refers to the true self buried in the impish din of psychic activity and "me" pretensions. It's not entirely clear what to make of Eckhart's "potential sensitivity," but it appears to be very much like what Weil says we discover in decreation: an original innocence unsullied by the accretions of the pretender self. The true self is a *potentiality* in the sense that it's an unfinished emptiness, unfilled with set-in-stone characteristics. It is a *sensitivity* because its emptiness is also an open receptivity and attentive availability. Thus the true self is both passive and active: passive because it awaits, but active because its mode of waiting implies an alert state of attentiveness free from distractions.

And what does the true self await? In a word, God. Silence and darkness, passive openness and active emptiness, is the place of encounter between the soul and divine mystery. The absolute nothingness of the desert God reaches out to embrace the decreated still point of the soul, and the two flow into one another like waters merging into the ocean.

This coming-together in silence and darkness is not so much communication as communion. Just as the Zen disciple and her koan commingle in the moment of enlightenment, so the soul and God do likewise. What was separated becomes united in a grand but darkly silent act of fusion. There is no longer "me" on the one hand and "God" on the other. As Eckhart says, "The eye with which I see God is the same eye with which God sees me; my eye and God's eye are only one eye and one seeing and one knowing and one love."[8]

Martin Buber calls the mystical fusion between the soul or true self and God *Begegnung. Begegnung* is usually translated as "meeting," but this rendering fails to capture the richness of the fusion. "Meeting" entails division: When two independent beings "meet," they come face-to-face with one another while still remaining separate. But *Begegnung* is more properly an interpenetration that melds two into one. When the soul and God enter into *Begegnung*, each becomes so totally present to the other that there is really only one presence, a "concentration and fusion," as Buber says, that leads to a "whole" state of being such that if the word "I" is uttered, so is the word "God."[9] Nothing can rupture the unity of *Begegnung,* because *Begegnung* occurs only in radical openness, and openness by definition is free of divisive distractions.[10]

But genuine *Begegnung,* as opposed to mere meeting, is only possible if the two that become one are already like one another. Disparates don't fuse; they only clash or, at best, stand opposite one another in uneasy détente. This means that the dark and silent still point of the true self must be like the dark and silent mystery of the desert God. Eckhart suggests as much in the earlier quoted passage where he says the soul's eye and God's eye are really identical. If they are identical, the implication is that the true self and God have always been one, but that something occurred to separate them from one another.

This insight immediately opens up three desert revelations for us. The first is that the fusion of *Begegnung* is not so much union as *re*-union. When soul communes with God, that which was originally one but subsequently splintered again becomes one. This is certainly Merton's opinion. In discussing the fusion that is "beyond words and...beyond speech and beyond concepts," he goes out of his way to add this:

> Not that we discover a new unity. We discover an older unity....[Soul and God] are already one, but we imagine that [they] are not. What we have to recover is our original unity. What we have to be—is what we are.[11]

So the interpenetration between soul and God that takes place after the "me" decreases in *tohu-bohu* is a recovery of lost oneness. This is the first revelation.

The second is that the original unity can only have been sundered by the destructive alienation Weil talked about in the previous chapter. Prior to our self-creation as noisily preoccupied "me's," our primal-state souls were as darkly still as the God from which they came. This is our true identity. But the emergence of ego cluttered the original openness of the true self with the encroachments of will, until the buzzing imps of psychic activity on the one hand and the imperious but delusional pretender self on the other ruptured the original unity. Only after the encroachments are swept away by the wind of *tohu-bohu,* only after the "me" contracts in *tsimtsum*—only after the two deaths of the desert reduce us to *ptoches*—do we rediscover our original "potential sensitivity," thereby clearing the ground for a recovery of unity.

The final revelation is the most mysterious of the three, one Buber has already hinted at it when he remarked that, after fusion, saying "I" is the same as saying "God." When *Begegnung* occurs, when dark silence interpenetrates with dark silence, what happens at the deepest, most unfathomable level, is that God embraces God. There is nothing in soul wilderness save God. The desert *is* God. And we who enter the desert to die—we, too, in our soul's core—are God. From the emptiness of the desert emerges a transformation infinitely more spectacular than Teresa d'Avila's birth of butterfly from cocoon. We go into the wasteland as persons and become there what we always were: God.

Nada, Nada, Nada

The claim that the desert allows such intimate communion between the soul and God that the soul *becomes* God is astounding. Some may even think it blasphemous. This is the fate of all religious koans. The entropic mind finds them

offensive stumbling blocks, and the desert koan is no exception. There's no way to defuse its paradoxicality, because
there's no way to tame the feral mystery of God. Still, a few
words can be said about God and the true self that might
move us a bit closer to the heart of the third desert revelation.

Most spiritual traditions agree that God is essentially
unknowable and hence ultimately unspeakable. At the same
time, they also concede that humans can symbolically gesture
at the dark and silent God through images, stories, poetry,
metaphors, and analogies. But such symbolic language
should never be taken as anything more than a woefully
inadequate stab at expressing what's fundamentally inexpressible. Otherwise we hazard conflating talk about God
with God—a species of the fallacy of misplaced concreteness
discussed in chapter 3.

The Christian mystical tradition has always worried
about this danger, and early on sought to by-pass it by
stressing the importance of going beyond worded or visual
images of God. As far back as the fourth century, Christian
mystics appealed to scripture and their own desert experiences to defend a spirituality that's come to be known as
"apophasis." The apophatic approach (apo="beyond";
phasis="image") teaches that all contrived images of God
inevitably get in the way of experiencing God, and that the
Godseeker must renounce them to achieve an immediate,
unifying Begegnung with the Divine. If the soul would know
the silent and dark God, it must grow silent and dark as
well. As John of the Cross put it centuries later, God is nothing, the way to God is nothing, and therefore the soul must
become nothing. Nada, nada, nada: the way, the means, the
goal. Only then can we experience God—and the experience, too, will be nada.[12]

But what sense can we make of the apophatic claim that God is *nada?* Obviously neither John of the Cross nor any other mystic wants to say that God doesn't *exist.* So what *do* they mean when they talk about the nothingness of God? In order to come to some idea of their intent, we may turn to Plato's discussion of *khora* in his dialogue *Timaeus.*[13]

Khora. Plato unexpectedly introduces *khora* in the middle of a rather commonplace metaphysical discussion of two realms of being: the sensible and the intelligible. When we survey reality, he says, we notice that it can be divided into physical things on the one hand and ideal or mental objects on the other. The physical realm, which we apprehend through the senses, is changeable. Material objects, whether natural or human-made, are subject to the passage of time and the accidents of location. By contrast, intelligible objects, knowable through reason, remain "always the same" because they're not similarly bound by time and space. The conceptual definitions and axioms that constitute geometry, for example, don't change. The intelligible realm supplies patterns for contingent objects in the physical realm— abstract lines, points, and planes provide the formal blueprints for concrete rocks, grass, and chairs—but those patterns aren't themselves contingent. They endure.[14]

Plato is dissatisfied with stopping here. He senses there must be another realm of reality, a "third kind of being...difficult of explanation and dimly seen," one that's neither sensible nor conceptual yet somehow generates and sustains both the physical and the intelligible worlds.[15]

Uncomfortably aware that he's launched into the uncharted waters of the unsayable, Plato deliberately invokes a fuzzily ambiguous term—*khora*—to put a name on what he's groping for. The most literal meaning of *khora* is probably "open space." The word was sometimes used by the Greeks to designate a public square or marketplace. But it has a more subtle meaning as well, and this is the one Plato especially wants to evoke: *khora* as the "invisible," the "formless," the "incomprehensible." Moreover, *khora* also carries connotations of the "mother," the "nurse," the "receptacle." *Khora* is the creative matrix that spawns objects, but is not itself a "this" or "that." It is mysteriously reflected in intelligible and sensible things, but is independent of them. It "provides a home" for "all created things" that are knowable and sayable, but itself "is an invisible and formless being" remaining "most incomprehensible." *Khora* is the third kind of being.[16]

Plato pulls back from actually calling *khora* "God."[17] But given what he says about its creative, sustaining, and independent nature, later Christian defenders of the apophatic way thought the identification a reasonable one. Like *khora,* the apophatic God exists, but does so "mysteriously," "invisibly," "formlessly," and "incomprehensibly." Like *khora,* God is a mothering absence, a nursing void, a creative open space that makes room for "thises" and "thats." Divine Being, in short, is totally unlike the being of either sensible or intelligible things, and this means that God essentially is nothing: Nothing. Objects, whether physical or intelligible, can be demarcated and defined by the senses or reason and hence known and spoken. This is what makes them objects. But nothing has no boundaries, emptiness no clear-cut parameters, and so is both unknowable and unspeakable. God—*Khora*—is forever hidden in darkness and silence.

Plato struggled against the limitations of philosophical language to say something about *Khora.* Centuries earlier, the author of the Chandogya Upanishad less stumblingly made the same point in the simple tale of Svetaketu and Uddalaka. Uddalaka, a Brahmin sage, is trying to teach his young son Svetaketu about the great divine nothingness. But after floundering for a while in the abstruse waters of philosophy, he realizes he's confused more than enlightened the lad. So Uddalaka switches strategies and instructs his son to bring him a fruit of the Nyagrodha tree. Svetaketu fetches the melon-like fruit and places it at his father's feet.

"Here it is, sir."
"Break it."
"It is broken, sir."
"What do you see?"
"Some seeds, extremely small, sir."
"Break one of them."
"It is broken, sir."
"What do you see?"
"Nothing, sir."[18]

This nothing, darkly and silently hidden away in the center of the Nyagrodha fruit as well as everything else, sensible or intelligible: This nothing, says Uddalaka, is God.

Darkness. Because divine *Khora* is no-thing, it is essentially dark.

Any object in the world, regardless of how obscure it may be, is potentially knowable through reason or the senses. The finitude of an object guarantees that the human mind can make at least some headway in understanding and defining it. Obscurity in the physical and intelligible realms dissolves under the spotlight of reason.

But the open desert of God has no azimuth by which to get a bearing. There are no circumscribed boundaries, no fixed edges to *Khora*. It is forever an uncanny mystery that defies classification. Even God's self-revelations are murky, shot through and through, as John Ruusbroec wrote, with "darkness, bareness, and nothingness."[19] *Khora* isn't simply obscure, as an unknown or little-known object is. *Khora* is darkly apophatic, beyond any image, and its darkness is impenetrable. Thus God, concludes the seventh-century Maximus the Confessor, is "unknowable and inaccessible to all and altogether beyond understanding."[20]

Both Hebrew and Christian scriptures speak in hushed tones of the desert God's darkness. When Yahweh reveals himself to Moses atop Sinai, the unconcealment, paradoxically, is also a concealing "thick darkness" (Exod 20:21), a smoky "cloud" enshrouding and hiding the mountain (Exod 24:15). Similarly, Yahweh's self-revelation to the despairing Job is so darkly incomprehensible that Job gives up trying to understand, bows his head, and concedes that the divine unconcealment "hides counsel without knowledge" (Job 42:2).

Christian spirituality revolves around the koan that God's most luminous revelation is the concrete person of Jesus. What could be more knowable than a touchable, seeable, hearable human being? But even here the unfathomable darkness of *Khora* baffles. Jesus the man's daily activities and words can be observed and recorded, but the divinity they radiate is forever elusive. The beloved disciple remarks that in spite of Jesus' historical presence, the spirit of truth within him is unknowable by the world (John 14:17). Paul says in his letter to the Romans (11:22) that the depth of God in Jesus is both "unsearchable" and "inscrutable." In the letter to Philippi (2:5–7), he elaborates: Even though Jesus is the clearest earthly revelation of God, that revelation is still mysterious because the very act of divine self-emptying accentuates God's hiddenness.

Jesus is the Nyagrodha fruit: Peel away the layers of his-
toricity and enfleshment, split open the seeds of his earthly
life, and what one finds is nothing. When we enter soul
wilderness, the desert wherein God dwells, the desert which
is God, we travel darkly through a dark land. Whoever
thinks a way can be lighted in the midst of desert darkness is
deceived. "If you have understood, then this is not God. If
you were able to understand, then you understood something else instead of God. If you were able to understand
even partially, then you have deceived yourself with your
own thoughts."[21]

Silence. Objects make noise. Clang them together and
they reverberate. Ideas clash with ideas, things grind against
other things. The noise of objects is one of the ways we come
to know them.

But *Khora* makes no noise. *Khora* is darkly unknowable,
and because it's unknowable it's also unnameable. *Khora* is
silent. Silence is the language of the desert God.

As devotees of the syllogistic god count on, names
inevitably seek to subdue and control. To name is to acquire
power over that which is named. A name pegs the named
down, freezes it with a label, neatly tucks it into a designated
slot. "When we give a thing a name," said Gregory of Nyssa,
"we imagine we have got hold of it. We imagine that we have
got hold of being." But *Khora,* he continues, is not a thing,
and so is nameless. Divine nothingness can't be tied down
with the Lilliputian ropes of language, and "we should do
better not to flatter ourselves too soon that we can name
God."[22] *Khora,* as the contemporary philosopher Jacques
Derrida says, is a *prénom,* a pre-name-ed silence.[23] This
insight accords with Eckhart's realization that "God, who

has no name—who is beyond names—is inexpressible."²⁴ (And "Who is Jesus?" asks Eckhart. "He [likewise] has no name."²⁵)

The desert God's unnameable silence, just like his darkness, is acknowledged in Hebrew and Christian scripture. When Yahweh darkly unconceals to Moses he appears as a bush that burns but is not consumed (Exod 3:2). A strange and wonderful image this, one of silent fire. Flame crackles only because the object on which it rides splinters and cracks as it combusts. But a flame that doesn't consume its object dances in deepest silence.

As if to underscore God's fiery silence, the author of Exodus also tells us that Moses was rebuffed when he tried to speak the silence (3:13-14). *Tell me your name,* Moses cried to the bush, *that I may tell it to the people of Israel.* But the great open space of God refused to be named. *Tell them I AM,* was the reply. *I AM:* Yahweh's acknowledgment that even he can't speak adequately of that which has no name.

When Elijah the prophet fled into the wasteland of Mt. Horeb to escape Jezebel's wrath, he likewise learned that the desert God is silent (1 Kgs 19:11-12). Standing on a crag of the mountain, Elijah sought evidence of God in Hollywood-ish special effects: windstorms that tossed about stones and trees, earthquakes that split open the earth's bowels, volcanic fires that evaporated the air. But God didn't speak in such strident tones. After the hurly-burly of natural cataclysm came the *kol demamah dakah,* the un-sound of sheer silence, and that un-sound was God's voice.

In the Christian Bible, Jesus is the archetypal conveyor of God's silence. This seems another paradox: After all, Jesus spends the final three years of his life speaking and speaking about the unspeakable God. But in this case the paradox is only apparent, for the mode of discourse preferred by Jesus is the indirect one of parabolic allegory. To speak allegorically is to utter one thing while meaning something else, something beyond the language actually used. Allegories arise from the unsayable and gesture back to it: "Words, after speech, reach/Into the silence."[26] Allegories circle around the unnameable, evoking its inexpressible depth, inviting the ears of the heart to heed what the senses and intellect can't pick up. Attending to the words of a parable at the expense of the silent spaces between them misses the point. When Jesus spoke parabolically of God, he sought to deafen us to human noise and awaken us to divine silence.[27]

At-(n)one-ment

We're now ready to hear as best we can Eckhart's attempt to speak the unspeakable truth that the darkly silent *Khora*—God—*is* our true self, our real identity, and that in the fusion of *Begegnung*, God reunites with God.

For Eckhart, the Incarnation is both an historical and an ongoing event. At a certain point in time, God self-emptied into the human Jesus of Nazareth and, as this human being, pitched his tent among us for thirty-odd years: the historical birth and life. But the self-emptying (or *tsimtsum*) that culminated in the Christ-event is recapitulated in every person: the ongoing incarnation, in which "God births his Son or the Word in the soul."[28] The deep core of the soul, a place of "central silence where no creature may enter, nor any idea," is where the Word dwells and dwells fully. "Here God enters the soul with all he has and not in part. He enters the soul through its core and nothing may touch that core except God himself," because the "core of the soul is sensitive to nothing but the divine Being, unmediated."[29]

This is a striking claim. What Eckhart suggests by it is that the soul is an open place, a clearing in the forest of creation that provides dwelling-room for the Divine. This doesn't mean, of course, that God is somehow "trapped" in the soul, any more than it implies that God's only "location" is in the soul. God is independent and limitless, existing both within and without the soul. What it does mean, however, is that the essence of personhood, what really makes us who we are—our *true* identity—is the dark and silent Word, or *Khora,* in the core of the soul.

Thus the original unity between God and soul: the first desert revelation.

But a human, although *essentially* soul, isn't *exclusively* soul. A person also possesses body and mind, and both begin clamoring for attention the instant we first draw breath. Neither are evil; they are part of God's creation, and God's creation is good. But they are unruly in their behavior and demanding in their appetites. These "agents," as Eckhart calls them, increase in volume and intensity, and begin laying down habitual patterns of response that move us progressively away from the indwelling Word and into the muck of entropy. Before long, the bio-psychological nexus the pretender self thinks it controls—ideas, will, imagination, sensation, emotions—has taken on a life of its own and pushes the *Khora*-core out of the range of our awareness. The core still remains our true identity, ever pulsing the "preconceptual apprehension" of God that Rahner says runs through all human experience. But it's now overpowered by the imperious "me," the false self we take as our true identity.

Thus the severing of the original unity: the second desert revelation.

To reestablish contact with the *Khora*-core, the self, as we've seen, must be "despoiled of all that [is] peculiarly [its] own."[30] It must become clean and featureless as a desert. In Eckhart's words,

> You must depart from all crowds and go back to the starting point, the core [of the soul] out of which you came. The crowds are the agents of the ["me"] and their activities: memory, understanding, and will, in all their diversifications. You must leave them all: sense perception, imagination, and all that you discover in self or intend to do.[31]

Eckhart knows that only the desert rescues us from the crowd. Only there can the two deaths mercilessly strip away the "nots"—not-soul, not-God, not-*Khora*, and so on—that stand between the soul and divine Being.[32] Simone Weil and Isaac Luria have helped us understand this dissolution as a *tsimtsum* which decreates the old self until we land in the between-stage of *tohu-bohu*. Then, when utter *ptoches* has emptied us of everything that ruptured the original unity and has restored us to the innocence of "potential sensitivity"— when, in other words, the soul reawakens to the no-thing it is—the grand fusion of *Begegnung* occurs, and God and the soul are at-one. Eckhart sums up the whole thing in characteristically homey language. "God asks only that you get out of his way, in so far as you are creature, and let him be God....[W]hen [you] have forsaken self, what remains is an indivisible union,"[33] or at-one-ment.

But notice what this at-one-ment means. The soul, restored to the *ptoches* of its original silence and darkness and hence neither nameable nor rationally knowable; the soul, a no-thing of open space, neither "this" nor "that"; the soul, an alert "sensitivity," a receptacle, a creative matrix in which spiritual birth takes place: This naughted soul has the mysterious characteristics of *Khora*. The soul, the true self, *is Khora*. When the pure nothingness of the soul embraces the pure nothingness of God, openness flows into openness, *Khora* merges with *Khora,* God returns to God.

The great act of at-one-ment—or, better, the great act of at-(n)one-ment, in which the nothingness of God-without unifies with the nothingness of God-within—is the wondrous restoration of our true identity. It is the "arrival," the completion, the fulfillment, that the desert had in store for us all along. In this overwhelming *Begegnung,*

> I discover that God and I are One. Now I am what I was and I neither add to nor subtract from anything, for I am the unmoved Mover, that moves all things....[Now] a man achieves the being that was always his and shall remain his eternally....I am changed into God and he makes me one with himself;...there is no distinction between us.[34]

Or as Gerard Manley Hopkins more dramatically put it in the nineteenth century,

> In a flash, at a trumpet crash,
> I am all at once what Christ is, since he was what I am,
>   and
> This Jack, joke, poor potsherd, patch, matchwood,
>   immortal diamond,
>   Is immortal diamond.[35]

God meeting God, immortal diamond recognizing its diamond nature: the third and greatest desert revelation.

Divine Naught

Eckhart's is the clearest (although still mysterious) insight we're likely to get into Jesus' death koan. *Ptoches* is *makarios* because it is both the way to God and the essence of God, and when we become *ptoches,* we enter into the ultimate enrichment. In at-(n)one-ment, "God is identical with the spirit [i.e., soul] and that is the most intimate poverty discoverable."³⁶ Blessed prosperity is a state of being, and no higher state than the utter nothingness of God is possible or imaginable.

At-(n)one-ment is the great secret of the desert, a mystery so incomprehensible and unimaginable that words and ideas and images can do no more than bow in speechless wonderment before it.

Eckhart's attempt to speak the unspeakable fusion of soul with *Khora* thrills the heart of the desert wanderer, but it shocks and offends homebodies. In the first place, his insistence on absolute destitution as the only way to recover innocence and discover God terrifies those of us who cling to the "me" of personal identity. Eckhart's vision of the soul's journey to the desert God is uncompromising: Either we die or we fail. In the second place, his insistence that "God and I are one" seems on the surface to be either a stunning example of hubris or a diffusion of God into an amorphously pantheistic nimbus. Church authorities in Eckhart's day certainly saw it as both and declared his writings heretical. (Shamefully, he still remains on the condemned list.)

Eckhart's language may be heterodox—this is only to be expected when one struggles to speak the mystery of a koan—but it's hardly heretical. His emphasis on death in the desert, for example, is entirely in keeping with the spiritual poverty taught by Jesus as well as subsequent Christian mystics. It only seems harshly forbidding to those who are confused about the nature of their own identities, who mistakenly assume that the pretender self rather than *Khora* is what they really are. Human identity is more suprapersonal than personal. The psychological "functions" of personality aren't what hold us together. Instead, they ride on our true center of gravity: *Khora*.

Moreover, the at-(n)one-ment is more panentheistic than pantheistic. Eckhart isn't claiming that God *is* everything, but rather that God is present *in* everything, and that the divine mode of presence is the nothingness of *Khora*. "God is Mind in all things," declares Eckhart, "and is more intimate to each than anything is to itself—and more natural."[37] The soul's heroic journey into the wilderness doesn't aim at merging with the cosmos. Instead, the point is to decreate so that the God who is imminent but hidden within the soul can appear.

Again, this seems perfectly consistent with both Christian scripture and the mystical tradition. Jesus, after all, proclaimed that the Kingdom of Heaven—that is, the place where God dwells—is already here (Luke 11:20; 17:20-21), and prayed that all people would enter that place to become one with God as he, Jesus, was one with God (John 17:20-23). Paul contended that God is within us (2 Cor 13:5) and that the desert adventure replaces the "me" with Christ: "It is no longer I who live, but Christ who lives in me" (Gal 2:20). John the Baptist, the shining light, the patron of all desert adventurers, concurred: In the desert, the "me" decreases so that the God who is our real identity—*Khora*—might increase (John 3:30).

Recall the Upanishadic story of Svetaketu and the Nyagrodha fruit. When young Svetaketu breaks open one of the seeds of the fruit and sees "nothing," his father explains to him that the nothing—"the subtle essence you do not see"— is God. But Uddalaka tells the lad something else as well. The

no-thing, the *Khora,* the open, receptive space, is also Svetaketu's true self. *Tat tvam asi,* Uddalaka says: "That art
thou." The divine naught which is in every created thing is
also in you, O Svetaketu, and it is your real identity. *That* is
what *thou* art. Thy soul is the *Khora* of God.[38]

This is what the desert whispers to us. This is the *makarios*
of *ptoches.* This is the rebirth that follows death.

Desert Freedom

When we die to the self and awaken to the indwelling God
in the mystical fusion of at-(n)one-ment, we arrive at the fulfillment we're destined for. We can become completely
human, as Simone Weil put it, only after we realize our God-
natures.[39] Prior to the *Begegnung* of soul and *Khora,* we are
subhuman, retarded in our spiritual growth by the pretender
self's fears and delusions. We dwell in a state of bondage to
our egoistic will, even though we fancy ourselves autonomous
and self-determining. We enslave ourselves to household
gods, even though we foolishly think we're in control of them.
But when the desert experience purges us of our illusions, it
also strikes off our chains and allows us to become what we
are meant to be. It frees us to soar higher even than Teresa's
butterfly. No wonder Eckhart exclaims, "I pray God that he
may quit me of god."[40]

The desert fathers and mothers knew the joy of freedom
at-(n)one-ment brings, and realized that it has two aspects.
The first is a freedom-from they usually styled *apatheia:* a
liberating indifference to the "me," to the snares of ego and
the bewitchments of personal identity. Who would pine for
stones when bread is available? Who could possibly have any
interest in the pretender self once the unimaginable depth of
the real self has been experienced? The habits and addictions

of the old self that once imprisoned us in entropic homes have dissolved in the desert sun, and the soul has become as uncluttered and unbound—"as young," chortles Eckhart—"as the day it was created."[41]

But there's also a freedom-to granted by soul wilderness, a freedom the desert mystics variously called *agrupnia* ("not-asleep"), *prosochi* ("attention"), or *nipsi* ("watchfulness"). As the awakening soul moves *away from* bondage to the pretender self's will, it grows *into* conformity with divine will. That will is boundless, unimpeded, and eternal. It is utterly "uncorrupted" by self-interest, observes Eckhart, and hence is absolutely "free."[42] It is pure receptivity, pure availability, pure openness, a continuous *agrupnia* that incorporates all creation. This should come as no surprise; Plato defined *Khora* as an open space of attentiveness. When the desert union of soul and *Khora* occurs, when we realize the God-nature of our true self, when our will fuses with divine will, the dynamic receptivity of God becomes ours and we are freed to be available to all creation.

Truly, as the Carmelite poet Jessica Powers observes, liberation is in the wilderness.[43] The wilderness monk Carlo Carretto agrees. "The exodus from slavery to freedom," he says, "takes place in the desert."[44]

The mystical freedom-to fusion of our will with God's leads to the final stage in the hero's spiritual journey: the prophetic return. The prophet is one who has learned to be silent so that God may speak through him or her.[45] And the divine voice that resounds in and through the prophet, the voice heard in the wilderness and carried back from the wilderness, is the voice of love. Love is the desert's daughter, said the hermit Evagrios Ponticus,[46] and when the desert traveler returns to civilization, so does the daughter.

Chapter Six

Voice from the Wilderness

By the roots of my hair some god got hold of me.
I sizzled in his blue volts like a desert prophet.
Sylvia Plath

Desert Bodhisattva

Karl Rahner's own version of the great Either/Or spells
out the options for spiritual wayfarers: either become a mystic or cease to be anything at all. We now know that a mysterious conjunction is hidden in Rahner's disjunction. If we
turn our backs on the desert, we destruct in the swamp of
spiritual entropy. But if we plunge into it, the "me" decreases
to vanishing point and we recover the freedom of *Khora*.
Either become a mystic *or* destruct: the disjunction. Become
a mystic *and* decrease to no-thing-ness: the conjunction. In
the first case, we cease to be anything of value; in the second,
we cease to value being a thing.

The desert sojourner no longer values unfree thinghood
when she turns her back on ju-ju *lares,* attains the unmediated experience of the Divine that is the goal of the mystical
way, and indwells the darkly silent desert koan. This is what

she was intended for. This is the end she made her way to all along, even if she didn't know it at the time. When she reaches it, she's "arrived."

But in her end is her beginning, for as the Baptist's example shows us, the mystic has a prophetic mandate to return to the world with tidings of her desert adventure. The spiritual hero's journey remains unfinished without this final step. Forsaking home, desert death, *Khora*-rebirth, *and* prophetic return—these are the necessary stages in the heroic quest.

One of the hallmarks of pseudo-spirituality is its emphasis on "contemplation" at the expense of "action." Too often mysticism is viewed by both would-be practitioners and outside observers as an unflappable quietism. On this reading, the mystic withdraws into a private hermitage, her own inner secret place, until she so loses contact with the external world that she grows completely detached from whatever may be happening in it. Involvement in mundane affairs only sullies the "higher state of consciousness" she's achieved. One can't be a contemplative Mary and a bustling Martha.

Such is the folk wisdom about the mystical way. But folk wisdom is as mistaken here as it is nearly everywhere else. Nothing is more foreign to genuine mystical enlightenment than a head-in-the-clouds distancing from the world. The spiritual hero doesn't leave home to spend the rest of her days in a cloister. On the contrary, she ventures into the desert so that she may eventually take its secret to her sisters and brothers. As Merton observed,

> We do not go into the desert to escape people but to learn how to find them; we do not leave them in order to have nothing more to do with them, but to find out the way to do them most good.[1]

Martha is perfectly compatible with Mary. The two sisters are one flesh and blood; their differences create a unified whole. Contemplation without action is self-indulgent narcissism; action without contemplation is the febrile hustling of a resumé-er. "What we plant in the soil of contemplation," says Eckhart, "we shall reap in the harvest of action." Only then is "the purpose of contemplation achieved."[2]

In the Mahayana Buddhist tradition, the exemplar of this kind of contemplative activity is the "Bodhisattva." A Bodhisattva is a person of enlightenment or at-(n)one-ment. (Obviously, all of us are potential Bodhisattvas; as we saw in the last chapter, *Khora* lies at the core of each soul.) Bodhisattvas have dwelt in the desert and discovered their true selves. But they "do not cling to the blissful taste" of the fusion by shutting themselves off from the rest of humanity. Instead, "with a great loving heart they look upon the sufferings of all beings" and, "filled with pity and love," voluntarily return to the world "to suffer themselves for the sake of those miserable beings."[3]

This return to the world is neither relinquishment nor repudiation of the desert rebirth, but rather an attempt to live it as a shining light for others. A Bodhisattva's move from the desert back into the world is "a single process" rather than a rupture. "If I go from one end of this house to the other, it is true, I shall be moving—and yet it will be all one motion."[4] Wilderness insight is carried to the public square; *Khora*-God flows into *khora*-marketplace; desert sand drifts into the nooks and crannies of home.

The Judaeo-Christian analogue to the Bodhisattva is the prophet. A prophet, observes Abraham Heschel, is one who brings to the world "attitudes *of* God rather than [just] ideas *about* God."[5] Anyone can talk about God in the abstract language of theology or philosophy. But only the mystic who has undergone desert at-(n)one-ment is able to communicate divine attitudes, because only she has experienced them firsthand. Thus a prophet, as Matthew Fox says, is a "mystic in action,"[6] an enlightened being who carries in her heart the unsayable desert Word to share with those who still linger on the other side of the great Either/Or.

But two questions immediately arise. First, why would an enlightened person *want* to return home? Even if we grant it's the right thing to do, what impels a desert sojourner to give up the blessedness of desert *ptoches* and dive back into a suffocatingly un-*ptoches* world? Second, what does it mean for the Bodhisattva/prophet to communicate "attitudes" of God rather than "ideas" about God? Obviously Heschel isn't referring here to the *prophet's* attitudes toward God, but *God's* actual attitudes. What does this signify?

We'll discover that both questions lead to one and the same answer.

Freedom to Love

In the last chapter we saw that at-(n)one-ment is liberating. It frees us from the "greedy greyhound" of the false self by reawakening us to our innate *Khora*-core. When God and the soul embrace in *Begegnung*, human will is restored to its original nature, and once again conforms to divine will. What was divided is now made whole.

But what's the essence of divine will? Our exploration of *Khora* has already suggested an answer. *Khora* is the open place, the no-thing, which is creatively available, nurturingly receptive. Plato's metaphorical references to it as "mother" or "nurse" are entirely appropriate. Like a mother, *Khora* brings us into being out of its own Being, sacrificially diminishing its plenitude for our sake. Like a nurse, *Khora* watches over us with solicitous care, continuously whispering the song of the desert in our hearts, coaxing us away from our sickbeds toward the health of at-(n)one-ment. Like both mother and nurse, *Khora* is always available to us, ready to receive us when we're ready to be received, eager to ground and sustain us.

What other name can one give this but "love"? Divine will is an unimpeded outward flow of love, and when our will is restored to its divine nature, we are freed to love as *Khora* loves.

One of the great ironies of life is that we think loving is the easiest thing in the world to do, when actually it's the most difficult. The false self cannot love, although it fancies otherwise. It only pretends to love, plays at being the great lover just as it plays at being in control of the psychic imps. Genuine loving requires freedom, and the ego is enslaved to its insecurities and pretensions, its ambitions and fears. It can never get out of its own way long enough to become the open place of nurturing receptivity from which love flows. It confuses neediness with availability and emotional ownership with intimacy.

How could it not? Dissonately driven by delusions of grandeur on the one hand and a nagging sense of vulnerability on the other, the pretender self is both too arrogant and too frightened to diminish for the sake of others, too impatiently fixated on its own desires to nurture someone else in need. Instead, its mode of loving requires others to diminish for *its* sake and forego their interests in deference to *its* desires. The predictable upshot of this self-centered playacting at love is hellish frustration for the false self as well as anyone unfortunate enough to be in relationship with it.

Enslavement is destructive even when the slave blithely denies his chains.

The desert sirocco rattles our shackles, forcing us to acknowledge them, and bondage-recognition, however reluctant it may be, is the first step to liberation. We begin the process of shedding the fetters when we say "yes" to the great Either/Or, and they fall off completely in the two desert deaths. The imperious, un-loving "me" contracts to vanishing point in *tsimtsum,* God reunites with God, and the *Khora* we've regained loves uninterruptedly through us. To love as God loves, to become open to others as God is, we must become nothing as God is nothing.

This is counter-intuitive. How can nothingness love or elicit love? Whatever else love is, surely it's a beneficent will to intimacy, a response from one thou to another thou, warmly personal and alive rather than abstractly impersonal. Yet the silent and dark *Khora* seems as cold as a metaphysical principle to many of us. We may accept that *Khora* is the creative source and sustaining foundation of all that is. We may have no trouble in agreeing that it cannot be a "this" or "that," and hence is no-thing. We may even concede that Luria's doctrine of divine shrinkage is a logical explanation of how the world came to be. But *tsimtsum* as an expression of love? No-thing-ness as a personal thou who gives and calls forth love? It seems too much to swallow.

If there's resistance to seeing *Khora* as a thou, it's probably because our pre-desert naiveté associates thou-ness with tangible, touchable, concrete bodies animated by "personality." To this way of thinking, a thou is a "me" almost as clearly defined as a physical object: I am a thou because I am a here-and-now embodied personality with a discernible identity all my own. Love occurs when two "me's" come into intimate contact with one another.

But such an understanding of the thou reduces humans to quasi-things—and things are impersonal its, never personal thous. What distinguishes the thou from an it is the elusiveness, the ungraspable ineluctability—the mystery—of the former. A thou is never just the sum total of psychic activity and spatio-temporal body; she's always much more than what she appears to be at any given moment. There's a fluid quality to the thou that can't be classified or collapsed into a set-in-stone it-identity: The personal, unlike the impersonal, always outstrips our attempts to define it. Embedded within the here-and-now concreteness of body and psyche is the transcendent nothingness of soul, and it's this that distinguishes a thou from an it. This nothingness, not the "me," is what's truly personal.

Moreover, only the elusive thou is capable of giving or eliciting genuine love. Concrete its, whether they're physical objects or "me"-objects, are beyond the pale of love. Love is an opening which beckons to the beloved, an availability that freely offers itself as a restorative haven, a receptivity that willingly makes room for others. Physical things, because of their nature, lack this opening; they're solid through and through. "Me"-things, because of their chronic insecurity, brick up the opening lest it make them vulnerable. In either case, love is an impossibility.

Thus the thou, the personal, isn't concrete personality so much as an elusive no-thing free of the rock-hard solidity of an it. When we think of a personal thou in this way, *Khora*, the ultimately dark and silent no-thing, reveals itself as ultimately personal Thou, capable of giving genuine love. When we fuse with *Khora* in the desert mystery of at-(n)one-ment, we too become thous and are liberated to love.

To return to our two questions: What's the divine attitude communicated by the prophet, and why does the prophet return? The answer to both is love. As radical openness, *Khora* is a Thou who opens to the universe in love. Love is the fundamental attitude of the Divine. The prophet's recovery of her *Khora*-nature fills her with an immediate experience of God's love, and this is the revelation she brings to others. But the prophet's self-emptying in the wilderness has also made her a thou participating in the divine Thou, and this means that she likewise participates in divine love. Love always and everywhere freely wills to open out to others in a receptive, available, and nurturing way. So the prophet returns, the Bodhisattva joyfully comes back, for the sake of love. Love is the cause and love is the goal. Dame Julian said it well: "Would you know your Lord's meaning...? Know it well: love was his meaning. Who showed it you? Love. What did he show you? Love. Wherefore did he show it you? For love."[7]

Loving Prophetically

The prophetic voice from the wilderness is God's voice, and that voice chants the song of love. Love is the divine attitude channeled through the prophet. Prophets may foretell future events, chastise corrupt social institutions, gadfly bovine complacency in individuals, or devote themselves to anonymous acts of charity. But the spirit that animates everything they do is *Khora,* and *Khora* is love.

Heschel tells us that the "ground-tone" of the divine love communicated by the prophet is "pathos."[8] This is a revealing statement. The Greek root of "pathos" is *pathein,* "to suffer." The root's Latin translation is *pati,* from which the

English "compassion" is derived. The essential attitude of divine love, then, is commiseration, fellow-feeling, empathy: a receptive compassion that opens out to embrace, share, and relieve the suffering of humankind.

We suffer, and we cause others to suffer, when our entropic frozenness alienates us from *Khora*. We deny who we are, pervert the natural course of our spiritual development, blight the well-being of our fellow humans and, in the words of John of the Cross, endure the bitterness of a life that "is no life at all."

But the suffering we inflict on ourselves and others redounds twice over on God. God suffers first because God is love and the ground-spring of that love is pathos. In observing the self-destructiveness of humanity, the God of infinite compassion cannot but partake in our suffering. But God suffers, secondly, because the wounds with which we mutilate ourselves also slash him. The indwelling *Khora* is perpetually crucified by the pretender self. The indissoluble union between soul and God necessarily means that whenever we foolishly strike a blow against ourselves, we also harm God. We are the limbs of God, as Paul says, and injury to a limb affects the entire body.

The implications of this are staggering, for they suggest that suffering is never isolated, never a private biological or psychological phenomenon. Instead, it always has cosmic ramifications. Every instance of suffering, regardless of how insignificant it may appear, rips the fabric of existence and ratchets up the overall level of destructiveness. Since suffering increases the sum total of alienation present in the universe, it implicates both God and persons. Suffering alienates us from God; suffering alienates God from us (as the Baal Shem Tov once said, the evildoer drives God into exile because the two "cannot live together in the same world"[9]); and suffering alienates the entire order of being from the wholeness for which it's destined.

But *Khora*-love is not just a compassionate suffering-with. It's also a nurturing response that seeks to heal what's been broken. In making itself available to the pain, *Khora* works from within to restore, willingly putting itself in harm's way in the hope of vanquishing alienation through at-(n)one-ment. This is the pathos-love the hero experienced in the wilderness, and when she returns she embodies it. Wedded to the desert's daughter, her mandate is to set love loose in the world to draw her brothers and sisters into the same salvific wasteland that slew and healed her. She comes to spark a revolutionary exodus from pharaoh's entropic kingdom. Like God, she will suffer for the sake of love: first because of her compassionate fellow-feeling, second because her revolutionary message will be resisted and attacked by the forces of entropy. She will be stoned by homebodies even as she grieves over the pain of their alienation from God. But in a broken world, this is the price paid by the prophet—and by God—for love.

The love practiced by the prophet, the love the prophet hopes to awaken in humanity, and the love which is *Khora*—for all are really one and the same—has four aspects: appreciation, compassion, challenge, and celebration.

Appreciation. According to Abraham Heschel, "the most important prerequisite of love is appreciation."[10] To love as God loves, one must first appreciate as God appreciates. Appreciation is a double movement that involves recognition on the one hand and gratitude on the other.

The pretender self quagmired in spiritual entropy looks at persons and sees them only as threatening "others." To it, they come across as greedy, grasping creatures perpetually conspiring to undermine its sovereignty. The syllogist fears and disdains the illiterate rabble, the orgy-porgyist worries that others might get in the way of his insatiable quest for emotional rushes, the codexer scorns humans as weak and wayward law-breakers, and the resumé-er laments the laziness of his fellows. The pretender self is surrounded by human filth on all sides, and burrows ever deeper into the isolation ward of its *lares* temple.

This black and bitter evaluation of humans is a delusion born from projection. As Carl Jung says, the pretender self casts its shadow on the world and thereby darkens it.[11] The ego's own private inferno of fear and anxiety and lust and anger and will-to-control becomes the filter through which it reads and distorts reality. Blindsided as it is by its own baleful nature, the pretender self fails to realize that when it detects hateful and hurtful qualities in others, it does so only because it possesses them itself.

But God's eyes are clear. God's vision is unimpeded by impish projections. God x-rays through entropic encrustations to discern the *Khora*-core, the potential sensitivity, in each human. God isn't blind to homebody alienation. His deep awareness of it is what lends pathos to his love. But the open clarity of *Khora* recognizes alienation as the fog that hides the pure no-thing-ness lying at the soul's core, and the core is what *Khora* focuses on. In looking at us, God also looks at himself.

When the prophet's old shadow-projecting self dies in the desert and her awakens to her *Khora*-core, her vision becomes transparent as God's. More precisely, her vision *is* God's: The *Khora* within her, the *Khora* that came to the fore in the great mystery of at-(n)one-ment, gazes through her eyes, and when *Khora* looks at other persons the prophet sees potential sensitivities. The prophet doesn't overlook the encrustation of impish pretense that smothers the soul, but—like God—knows it to be facade rather than substance. She focuses on the good—on the God—in each person.

This penetrating vision is the "appreciation" Heschel names as the prerequisite for genuine loving. As the Latin root of "appreciate" suggests, it's a recognition of the true *value,* the genuine *worth,* of persons. The prophet recognizes that what surrounds her is not human filth but embodied and supremely lovable *Khora.* C. S. Lewis once remarked that we ought to tremble in awe whenever we stand before another person, because he or she is no mere mortal but a spark of the Divine.[12] God is observable in the faces of our fellows, even when those faces are besmeared. The prophet appreciates this great mystery.

Denise Levertov wonderfully evokes the idea of prophetic recognition in a parable about a caterpillar (a poetic symbol for humankind) she encounters on a busy sidewalk. The creature is "shiny, hairless, not cute,...a mixture of millipede and scorpion." It's color is "repulsively fecal," and it looks dangerous: "[I]t may sting." On the surface, nothing seems redeeming in this repellent little life-form. But underneath its ugly top soil, Levertov senses a core of holiness, of sacredness, worthy of love and veneration:

> ...scoop it carefully
> into your hands,
> take it to safety! Not cute, not cute,
> it shrinks as you move to meet it,
> don't let it vanish before you have time
> to give it your heart, a work of mercy.[13]

The caterpillar's appearance remains ugly; that hasn't changed. But Levertov's recognition-ability to look beyond the obvious allows her to love, to give her heart, to perform a work of mercy, for the sake of the holiness hidden in the ugliness. This is the first moment of prophetic appreciation.

The second is gratitude. The prophet's recognition of *Khora* in other persons fills her with an awed sense of thankfulness for the riches—the "immortal diamonds," as Hopkins says—that surround her. Everywhere she looks, goodness; everyone she meets: God. She passes God on busy sidewalks, she sups with God at fast food restaurants, she touches God in even the most cursory handshake. The prophet's ordeal in the desert has removed the scales from her eyes, and she now sees that the world is saturated with the nothingness of God, that the stitchwork holding the fabric of existence together is *Khora*. Every human being is an occasion for falling to her knees and giving thanks, because every human being is *Khora*. *Tat tvam asi.*

How wonderfully surprised and awed and grateful the Baptist must've been when he stumbled out of the great desert emptiness of God only to recognize that the bustling and noisy world of humans is God as well. Nothing short of the mystical fusion in the wilderness, which allows us to become the *Khora* we always were and thus see through God's eyes, grants this transparency of vision. Humanistic credos, abstract arguments defending the dignity of persons, sentimental gushings about the goodness of humans: None of these will foster, much less sustain, a deep-down appreciation for the sacred beings caterpillar-persons really are. Recognition and gratitude are gifts of the spirit, not the intellect or the emotions, and we must go to the desert to receive them.

Compassion. A corollary of folk wisdom's belief that mysticism sacrifices action for contemplation is its impression that the attainment of union with God somehow rules out "feelings." The mystic sits in solitude atop her misty mountain top and gazes with cool equanimity on the rest of humankind, indifferent to either the joys or sufferings of the crowd.

This, of course, is nonsense. It's true that the desert has exorcised the imps of unbridled, self-centered emotions that once plagued the mystic; but this decreation doesn't leave her a coldly aloof spectator. In losing the pretender self to the sirocco, the mystic at-(n)ones with the great receptivity of *Khora,* a receptivity which, we've seen, is both personal and loving. "The first outburst of everything God does," says Eckhart, "is compassion."[14] Coming into her own *Khora*-nature allows the mystic to share in the compassionate receptivity of God—to burst out, like the desert rose, as a thou able and willing to empathize with suffering humanity.

Moreover, the mystic's own wilderness scourging has fine-tuned her sensitivity to the alienated suffering of others. She's been where they are; she's experienced the suffocating oppressiveness of the labyrinth, the panicked paralysis at the prospect of falling into *tohu-bohu.* She's stared into the faces of the demons who enslave her brothers and sisters, because they're the same ones who held her in bondage as well. She has first-hand knowledge of the misery of a soul trapped in entropic destructiveness, and this knowledge draws her heart even closer to fellow-sufferers. When the mystic returns as prophet, she is decreatively detached from the snares of pretender self emotions; this is the freedom of *apatheia.* But her wilderness trial has awakened an empathic attentiveness to the misery ego continues to inflict on others: the freedom of *agrupnia.*

Mystical liberation, then, is not incompatible with prophetic sensitivity. Mystics aren't barren of "feelings"; in fact, their self-emptying is precisely the crucible for the emergence of genuinely heartfelt empathy. When they return from the desert, says Merton, they come back with their "capacity for feeling expanded and deepened, strengthened against the appeals of falsity, warned against temptation, great, noble and pure."[15]

This spiritualized "capacity for feeling" the prophet brings to the world is a reflection of the pathos Heschel calls the ground tone of God's love. Just as *Khora* stretches out to embrace, suffer with, and suffer for humanity, so the *Khora*-awakened prophet's ministry likewise has compassion as its center of gravity. She willingly renounces the blissful isolation of the desert to re-enter the unpredictable and demon-fraught world and throw her lot in with her fellows. She opens wide her arms, inviting them to ease their burden of alienation by giving some of it to her. She offers herself up as a sacrifice for the world's pain, first because she willingly shares its suffering, second because she hazards the rebukes and blows of entropy-stiffened homebodies. Out of loving compassion, the divine compassion that now saturates her very being, she humbly submits to utter vulnerability for the sake of alienated humanity. Just as she diminished in the desert so that *Khora* could increase, so now, back in the world, she willing contracts in self-giving *tsimtsum* so that others might increase.

For *tsimtsum* is the consequence of loving as God loves. The reward of prophetically compassionate love is the *ptoches* that is *makarios*. When the soul at-(n)one with God loves, it replays the radical shrinkage experienced in the desert, which in turn is a recapitulation of *Khora's* perpetual self-emptying—perpetual impoverishment—for the sake of creation. This is what a thou does when a thou loves. As Johann Metz wisely says, "every stirring of genuine love makes us poor. It dominates the whole human person, makes absolute claims upon him, and thus subverts all extra-human assurances of security." Only this acceptance of radical vulnerability on the part of the prophet "lets the other person approach" near enough to hear the word she brings.[16] And that word is the desert Word, the same Word the prophet herself got close enough to hear when she died the two deaths of the wilderness.

Other persons can approach the prophet only if she goes to where they are instead of insisting that they come to her. This is the reason she forsakes the desert to return to the world. But the return is only the first step in getting close to sufferers. It must be followed by an immersion on the prophet's part in the ordinary lives of the people she yearns to touch.

The *Khora*-message of compassionate love is sometimes proclaimed to excitable multitudes or to haughty kings and queens, and biblical stories about prophets typically focus on such spectacular scenes. One thinks of Moses in pharaoh's court, Elijah's showdown with the Baalites, Jeremiah's trumpeting to the masses, the Baptist's voice ringing across the crowd-packed river gorge.

But usually the *Khora*-love the prophet brings to the world is both expressed and lived in quieter, more anonymous ways. The quotidian, the commonplace routine of existence, is the place most people dwell, and it's to that place the prophet brings her compassion. Auditoriums and sound systems, Father Urban-like marketing, or combustive razzmatazz in glass cathedrals aren't needed. The everyday round of work, conversation, meal-sharing, child-rearing, and errand-running provides ample opportunity for God to love through the prophet.[17] As the nineteenth-century hymnist John Keble said in a slightly saccharine but nonetheless insightful verse,

> The trivial round, the common task,
> Will furnish all we ought to ask;
> Room to deny ourselves, a road
> To bring us daily nearer God.[18]

Participating in the common life of ordinary individuals, self-emptying into the everyday just as *Khora* self-empties into each ordinary human being, the prophet's living example of compassionate love works from within to transfigure the ordinary.

Actually, this transfiguration is an unconcealment. As we've already noted, there is no "ordinary." God's wind, the liberating and vitalizing desert sirocco, blows within the most boring routine and monotonous existence. Soul wilderness is the place where *Khora* dwells, and soul wilderness is here, now, in the midst of the commonplace, in spite of its concealment by entropy. The prophet's living message of love, her shining example of the *makarios* of *ptoches,* her day-by-day dying for the sake of bringing others to life, loosens the bonds of alienation that block the wind from rising up in the midst of the ordinary. Love is the catalyst that allows the ordinary to unconceal as extraordinary.

When prophetic love—*Khora*-love—transfigures the quotidian in this way, the everyday world ceases to be an entropic swamp and becomes a vehicle of grace that, Karl Rahner says, makes us "free from ourselves as nothing else can." That which earlier seemed most earthbound enables us "to soar out into the infinite expanses of God in longing and holy desire and also take along all the lost things of the everyday as a song of praise of the divine splendor." Then, he concludes, "the entire everyday becomes the breathing of love, breathing of longing, of loyalty, of faith, of readiness, of devotion to God....Then all going out into the world, the everyday, becomes a going into God's unity, which is eternal life."[19]

Rahner's words bring us back to Heschel's notion of "appreciation," the prerequisite of genuine love. Compassion isn't possible unless we see humans as *Khora* sees humans: bearers of the divine enslaved to their pretender selves. The prophet's transfiguration of the ordinary nurtures the insight of appreciative self-recognition in those with whom she lives. Her example of self-giving love opens up for them a window into their own *Khora*-cores, their true selves. It starts them on the path of discovery that leads away from captivity to the freedom of desert at-(n)one-ment.

Challenge. A Bodhisattva from the desert is restless until the homebodies to whom she brings the desert wind likewise take the plunge into soul wilderness. But she knows from personal experience that most of them will resist crossing over into that dreadful ego-killing place. Years of spiritual entropy plug the ears and harden the heart, insulating the homebody from everything but the incessant demands of the pretender self.

The prophet's living example of compassionate love can begin to thaw the ice caves that encase entropic hearts. Her daily self-emptying and suffering-with can plant the seed of *Khora*-recognition in the pretender self's tundra, enabling those who hear the spoken and lived Word she brings to take a few steps toward questioning their own existence. But if the prophet stops here, chances are good that the freezing effects of spiritual conservatism will reassert themselves, the seed will fail to flourish, and the captives she's come to liberate will sink back into their dungeons. Very few of us enter the desert willingly. None of us do so joyfully.

So the prophet realizes that her shining example of *Khora*-recognition, *Khora*-gratitude, and *Khora*-compassion must be complemented by the sterner stuff of challenge. Like the Baptist, she speaks words that drive daggers through the hearts of her audience, harsh words that expose *lares* for the rusted gods they are and call into question the deluded pretensions of the false self. From the standpoint of homebodies, the prophetic message is a hateful, hurtful one. Merton evokes both its horror and its potential for awakening *Khora*-awareness—which is precisely why it's so horrible to the pretender self—when he poetically imagines John the Baptist thundering these words of challenge at the crowd:

> This is the day that you shall hear and hate
> The voice of the beloved servant.
> This is the day your scrutiny shall fear
> A terrible and peaceful angel, dressed in skins,
> Knowing it is your greedy eyes, not his, that die of hunger.[20]

Prophetic challenge, then, is prophetic denunciation of home—not for the sake of mere condemnation, but in the hope that as the fairy palace bewitchment of home becomes more apparent, receptivity to the desert will grow. We saw in chapter 3 that most of us refuse to forsake home until we become agonizingly aware of its labyrinthine nature. Prophetic challenge pushes us in that direction by forcing us to see, as Walter Brueggemann puts it, that the only way to receive is to relinquish, only grief permits newness, only shame brings liberation.[21]

Soul Wilderness

Karl Rahner asserted that it takes the despair of a "decisive moment" to jolt most of us out of our homebody stupor. This decisive moment, when it comes, is a grace given by God alone. But the prophet is an instrument of grace, a conduit through which *Khora* works in the world. So prophetic challenge is one of the means by which God seeks to demolish our old lives in a decisive moment.

Prophetic *Khora* does this by lobbing fragmentation bombs at us. As the example of John the Baptist shows, these bombs are aimed straight for the heart, and each one that hits tears away yet another chunk of entropy illusion. The volley is relentless; accusations and denunciations rain down in one fiery jeremiad after another. The homebody hunkers down in her *lares* bunker, angry and frightened but defiantly banking that its ironclad walls will hold.

The great irony, of course, is that they do—in a manner of speaking. For the prophetic bombardment isn't intended to explode the bunker so much as to drive the homebody so deeply into its recesses that what once appeared home now reveals itself as an airless, suffocating prison: the labyrinth. Sooner or later the atmosphere becomes so intolerable that the homebody, numb with confusion, paralyzed by a sense of helplessness, sickened with spiritual claustrophobia, realizes the only option left her is the great Either/Or. The decisive moment has reached its climax: Stay and smother or surrender and leap—into the desert abyss.

Prophetic challenge strikes many of us as horribly cruel and viciously judgmental. We cringe when we read biblical stories of prophets blasting their peers with white-hot denunciations. Surely, we tell ourselves, this level of verbal violence and name calling is unnecessary. Surely, also, there's something suspicious about the unrelenting intensity of it all; one begins to suspect that a Joel or Jeremiah (or the Baptist, for that matter) self-righteously revels in vituperation.

But before we rush to this judgment, we ought to keep a couple of points about prophetic challenge in mind.

The first is that prophetic harshness is born from love rather than holier-than-thou spleen. The prophet gets no more pleasure from pushing us toward the dreadful decisive moment than God derives from killing us in the desert. Love wishes to alleviate suffering, not cause it. But love also knows that pain is often a necessary prelude to *Khora*-discovery. Recognizing one's home as a labyrinthine fairy palace is always an ordeal, but without it there's no home-leaving, no venture into soul wilderness, and no at-(n)one-ment. The prophet knows this, and blasts away until the *lares* begin to totter. He inflicts pain for the sake of love. He practices what Kathleen Norris perceptively calls "holy wickedness."

Norris reminds us that the word "wicked" originally had a more benign meaning than it carries today. A "wickedness" wasn't an evil act so much as a course of behavior intended to bend or change or weaken. Thus a "wise-woman" would "cast a 'wicked' spell in order to bend a lover's heart to fall in love, to change another's mind, or to weaken an enemy."[22]

Norris thinks we need to re-embrace the ancient meaning of the word by recognizing that "there is such a thing as holy wickedness...undertaken wholly for the good."[23] The attitude of holy wickedness accepts the necessity that immediate pain and suffering may be necessary catalysts for genuine long-term well-being. It's "wicked" because it frequently stirs up "emotional mayhem." But it's "holy" because it wishes the mayhem only for the sake of the good.[24]

The example of holy wickedness Norris gives nicely illustrates her point. A small community of nuns she knew was threatened with eviction. Their convent was on the property of a parish church pastored by a Father Urban-type priest with big plans for renovation and expansion, and the plans didn't include Norris's nuns. Everyone was opposed to the priest's empire-building: parishioners, the community at large, the church staff, and of course the nuns. But the priest was adamant. As one of the sisters told Norris, "He doesn't listen well. He thinks if he wants it, it should happen."[25]

This same nun finally felt she'd reached the end of the line. Rational persuasion hadn't brought the priest to his senses, and prayers for his conversion weren't getting anywhere either. So the meek and mild sister threw her bombshell. She decided that the strong medicine needed was for the priest to fall in love, and accordingly prayed for this to happen. As she explained,

> Not that he run out and have an affair, but that he learn what it is to listen, to be attentive, to want to hang on to every word. I don't think he's ever been in love. And I want to see him totally vulnerable, the way we are when we fall head over heels.[26]

Although her modesty may have resisted the comparison, the nun was engaging in a holy wickedness every bit as inspired as the denunciations of the great biblical prophets. She came to the realization that the only way for the priest to be liberated from his ironclad entropy was through the grinding into fine dust an experience of total vulnerability like genuine love brings. Her expression "falling head over heels" is particularly appropriate: We awaken to the arrogance of ego only when the home turf is jerked out from under us and we fall into the abyss of misery. This is what the good sister wished for the priest—not because she bore him ill-will, but because she longed for his emancipation—and this is the goal of all prophetic challenge.

The second point to keep in mind about prophetic bombardment is that it brings no joy to the prophet. On the contrary, it burdens her with even more suffering. Vehicle of *Khora*-compassion that she is, the prophet wishes only to ease distress and bring freedom. The infliction of suffering on others, regardless of motive or consequence, is repugnant to her. The parent who lovingly chastises a child, the wife who lovingly rebukes her husband, does so for the good of the child and spouse, even though the holy wickedness self-inflicts the pain of causing others pain. Surely this is one of the reasons so many prophets balked at the divine summons: *Who am I to tell the people how to live?* they protested. *Why do you call me, a mere cutter of sycamore trees, to this task?* Such timidity is at least partly a resistance to the prospect of hurting others, even for their own good. So the prophet doesn't revel in her jeremiads. They're yet another empathic acceptance of suffering, yet another *tsimtsum* stripping-down, which both reflects and embodies the *Khora*-message of love.

Celebration. The fourth aspect of prophetic love both runs through the other three and is their culmination. It is celebration, the exuberantly laughing, dancing, merry-making joy that always accompanies love, even a love whose fundamental attitude is pathos.

The prophet looks at the world around her and appreciates it for what it is: God-saturated. This is an occasion for festive celebration. She empathically enters into the suffering of souls alienated from God, and her anticipation of the freedom and fulfillment that awaits them when they make their way through the desert also evokes a celebratory mood. The prophet challenges them to open their hearts to the decisive moment, and when they do, this too is cause for merriment. And when the level of destructiveness drops and the level of decreative at-(n)one-ment rises; when all creation moves closer and closer to loving fusion with the Creator; when the presence of *Khora* increases and the silent sands steadily blow their way into the world until there's no longer anything but desert: This is the greatest cause for celebration and laughter and joy. For then *Khora* becomes what it always was—all in all—and humans attain what they were always intended for—unity with God.

The prophet sees these causes for celebration, even if they're not obvious to homebodies, because the prophet gazes through *Khora's* eyes, and *Khora* sees not only what is, but also what should and will be. Joy is inseparably intermingled with pathos in divine love. God is not merely the sober God of compassionate sorrow; he is also the happy God of gleefully expectant laughter. Karl Rahner put it well:

> God laughs. He laughs the laughter of the carefree, the confident, the unthreatened. He laughs the laughter of divine superiority over all the horrible confusion of universal history that is full of blood and torture and insanity and baseness. He laughs sympathetically and knowingly, almost as if he was enjoying the tearful drama of this earth (he can do this, for he himself wept with the earth, and he, crushed even to death and abandoned by God, felt the shock wave of terror). He laughs....[27]

When the prophet joins in the divine belly-laugh, she does so because her soul-core is filled with celebratory *Khora*-love. That's why Rahner goes on to say that human laughter is

an image and a reflection of the triumphant, glorious
God of history and of eternity, [shining] in the final
laugh that somewhere springs out from a good heart,
bright as silver and pure, over some stupidity of this
world. Laughter is praise of God because it is a gentle
echo of God's laughter.[28]

One of the surest giveaways of entropic religiosity is its
dour and deadly seriousness. This jaw-clenching earnestness
is especially apparent in devotees of the syllogistic, codex, and
resumé gods, but it lies just beneath the surface with orgy-
porgyists as well: Their desperately frenetic choreographing
of emotional rushes is anything but playful. Whenever religion becomes an exclusively serious affair, it loses touch with
the *Khora*-love that ought to be its foundation and impetus.
This isn't to say that religion should be cavalier about the very
real suffering of humanity or the alienated brokenness of the
world, but only that it joyfully and hopefully attunes to the
Khora-promise of redemptive at-(n)one-ment as well.
Humans are vehicles of the laughing, loving God and as such
should lovingly laugh themselves. It's not insignificant that
Jesus' public ministry was launched at a wedding, a joyfully
merry celebration of love. "God gave us laughter," says Rahner; "we should admit this and—laugh."[29]

The prophet knows how to laugh, and she wishes to help
others learn to laugh as well. To do that, she first teaches them
the other steps of love: They must appreciate, as she does, the
Khora-nature of all humans; they must be compassionate
toward alienated suffering wherever it's discovered; and they
must accept the challenge of the great Either/Or. Only then,
after they've ventured forth into soul wilderness and disap-
peared in the dreadful death koan, are they liberated to emerge
as fellow-Bodhisattvas, ready to join in the cosmic guffaw of

sheer joy. Laughter, like love, is an unimpeded flow of free-dom, and freedom is found only in the desert.

Japanese and Chinese prints of Zen or Taoist sages are curious. The sages frequently have uncanny expressions on their faces that wed heavy-browed scowls of pain with sparkling-eyed laughter. This dissonance is striking, and gives the sages the appearance of madness. But the portraits in fact are visual koans, and they reflect the nature of the *Khora*-love discovered in the paradoxical desert. The mys-tery of at-(n)one-ment doesn't take away the dreadful nature of the death koan, but it does reveal another of its aspects: celebratory joy. When we fuse with *Khora* and become one with the death koan, when we live the *ptoches* that is *makar-ios*, we live its dread and joy as well. In an earlier chapter I suggested that we must imagine Jesus thundering the horrible death koan in his Sermon on the Mount with dancing eyes and smiling lips. Now we see why. Jesus the riddler, Jesus the great Koan, Jesus the supreme Bodhisattva, knows the secret of desert love.

Electric Madness

The crazed features given to Taoist and Zen sages are well-placed: Prophets *are* mad, just as poets are mad. As Sylvia Plath says, they've been seized by the blue voltage of God, and the intensity of their visionary shock has driven them over the edge, exiled them from the realm of the ordi-nary, transformed them into revolutionary heretics. Vacated in the service of their electric God, they are sensi-tive to nothing but the song they sing. But because the song is mysteriously unsingable, they will explode their hearts in the trying, and from the hurtling shards new worlds are born.

Plato said the poet is "a light and winged thing...seized with Bacchic transport," and his verse "divine and from the gods." Thus poets are "nothing but interpreters of the gods, each one possessed by the divinity to whom he is in bondage."[30] In speaking the dark and silent language of God, the poet becomes a lodestone that attracts others and "imparts" or passes on to them the inspiration that crackles in him. The ring of blue electricity extends ever outwards until all of creation is joined in one grandly throbbing energy field.

The same can be said of the mystic-prophet. As the Hebrew suggests, a prophet *(nabi)* is one who "bubbles forth" *(naba)* with the spirit of God. Liberated from the clay of the pretender self, the divine pulsation of *Khora* flows in and through her to shoot its voltage to all the world. Her electrifying message is not simply about *Khora:* It *is Khora.* She has shrunk to no-thing in soul wilderness, and in becoming no-thing has become *Khora.* She, like John, like the laughing sages—like that lunatic Godman Jesus—has lost her mind in the service of God.

Such lunacy is blessed, for it is mystical destitution. Such lunacy is blessed, for it is prophetic revolution. Such lunacy is blessed, for it is salvific. Another paradox from the koanic desert, another reason the Taoist sage laughs: The only persons wise enough to collaborate in the redemption of creation are fools.

> Only these lunatics (O happy chance)
> Only these are sent.[31]

May we all be seized by the electric God and crackle in his mad desert embrace.

Notes

Chapter One.

The chapter epigraphs are from Robert Frost, "Desert Places," in *The Poetry of Robert Frost,* ed. Edward Connery Lathem (New York: Henry Holt, 1979) and Rainer Maria Rilke, "Lament" in *Selected Poetry,* trans. Stephen Mitchell (New York: Vintage, 1989).

1. T. S. Eliot, "The Hollow Men," in *Complete Poems and Plays, 1909–1950* (New York: Harcourt, Brace & World, 1971), p. 57.

2. Geoffrey Morehouse, *The Fearful Void* (New York: Clarkson N. Potter, Inc., 1974), p. 257.

3. Thomas Merton, *New Seeds of Contemplation* (New York: New Directions, 1961), p. 81.

4. *The Letters of William Butler Yeats,* ed. Allan Wade (New York: Macmillan, 1955), p. 922. The passage is from a letter Yeats wrote 4 January 1939, two weeks before his death.

5. William Johnston is especially good at pointing out the koanic nature of Christianity. See his *Christian Zen* (San Francisco: Harper & Row, 1979) and *Silent Music* (San Francisco: Harper & Row, 1976). Also insightful are Donald W. Mitchell's *Spirituality and Emptiness: The Dynamics of Spiritual Life in Buddhism and*

Christianity (New York: Paulist Press, 1991) and "Buddhist and Christian Postmodern Spiritualities," in *Divine Representations: Postmodernism and Spirituality,* ed. Ann W. Astell (New York: Paulist Press, 1994), pp. 129–48. Finally, Thomas Merton's exchange with D. T. Suzuki in *Zen and the Birds of Appetite* (New York: New Directions, 1968), pp. 99–138, is helpful.

6. Meister Eckhart, *Sermon 28,* in *Meister Eckhart: A Modern Translation,* trans. Raymond B. Blakney (New York: Harper, 1941), p. 229.

7. Origen, *Homily XXVII on Numbers,* in *Origen,* trans. Rowan Greer (New York: Paulist Press, 1979), p. 268.

8. Campbell discusses the transformative dynamics of the hero's journey in many of his writings, but the *locus classicus* is *The Hero with a Thousand Faces,* Bollingen Series XVII (Princeton: Princeton University Press, 1949).

9. Gerard Manley Hopkins, "No worst, there is none," in *Poems and Prose of Gerard Manley Hopkins,* ed. W. H. Gardner (New York: Penguin, 1984), p. 61.

10. Teresa d'Avila, *Interior Castle,* trans. E. Allison Peers (New York: Image, 1994), p. 106.

11. Thomas Merton, *The Journals of Thomas Merton.* Vol. 3: *A Search for Solitude,* ed. Lawrence S. Cunningham (San Francisco: Harper, 1997), p. 318.

12. Teresa d'Avila, *Interior Castle,* p. 106.

13. Psalms of Solomon, Ode 11, in *The Other Bible: Jewish Pseudepigrapha, Christian Apocrypha, Gnostic Scriptures, Kabbalah, Dead Sea Scrolls,* ed. Willis Barnstone (San Francisco: Harper, 1984), p. 273.

14. For a short but insightful treatment of scriptural interpretations of desert/wilderness, see Ulrich W. Mauser, *Christ in the Wilderness* (Naperville, IL: Alec R. Allenson, Inc., 1963).

15. The more things change the more they stay the same. Thirteen hundred years later, when the English mystic Richard Rolle sought to emulate John by retreating into a secluded hermitage and exchanging his luxurious clothes for a simple habit, his sister likewise mistook soul wilderness for psychosis. *Frater meus insanit,* she lamented: "My brother's gone mad." *Richard Rolle: The English Writings,* trans. & ed. Rosamund S. Allen (New York: Paulist Press, 1988), p. 9.

16. Karl Rahner, "Christian Living Formerly and Today," in *Theological Investigations* VII (New York: Seabury Press, 1972), p. 15.

17. *Karl Rahner in Dialogue: Conversations and Interviews, 1965–1982,* eds. Hubert Biallowons, Harvey D. Egan, Paul Imhof (New York: Crossroad, 1986), p. 182.

18. Edmond Jabès, *The Book of Resemblances.* Vol. 2: *Intimations of the Desert,* trans. Rosmarie Waldrop (Hanover, NH: Wesleyan University Press, 1991), p. 1.

19. Karl Rahner, *Foundations of Christian Faith,* trans. William V. Dych (New York: Crossroad, 1989), p. 403.

Chapter Two.

The chapter epigraph is from Mary Oliver, "Some Questions You Might Ask," in *New and Selected Poems* (Boston: Beacon Press, 1992).

1. Yevgeny Zamyatin, "On Literature, Revolution, Entropy, and Other Matters," in *A Soviet Heretic: Essays,* ed. & trans. Mirra Ginsburg (Chicago: University of Chicago Press, 1975), p. 108.

2. Ibid.

3. The entropic freeze of northern hemisphere religiosity is especially emphasized by liberation theologians such as Gustavo Gutierrez, Leonardo Boff, and Juan Luis Segundo. They're struck by

Soul Wilderness

how North American and European theologizing over the last two
hundred or so years has centered around academic questions of
whether God exists, rather than the pressing issue of living the gospel
message of justice and peace in a broken world. Their conclusion is
that the self-doubting and abstract escapism of northern hemisphere
religiosity suggests a spiritual jadedness characteristic of religious
entropy. This sentiment is echoed by Johann Metz, who worries that
Europe and North America suffer from "a weariness with God." See
Ekkehard Schuster and Reinhold Boschert-Kimmig, eds., *Hope
Against Hope: Johann Baptist Metz and Elie Wiesel Speak Out on
the Holocaust* (New York: Paulist Press, 1999), p. 8.

    4. Abraham Heschel, *God in Search of Man: A Philosophy of
Judaism* (New York: Noonday Press, 1997), p. 3.

    5. Søren Kierkegaard, *Practice in Christianity*, trans. Howard
V. Hong & Edna H. Hong (Princeton: Princeton University Press,
1991), p. 67.

    6. Jacques Ellul, *The Subversion of Christianity*, trans. Geof-
frey W. Bromiley (Grand Rapids, MI: William B. Eerdmans, 1986),
p. 172.

    7. Elizabeth Bishop, "Jeronimo's House," in *The Complete
Poems, 1927–1979* (New York: Farrar, Straus and Giroux, 1999),
p. 34.

    8. Hermann Hesse, *Narcissus and Goldmund,* trans. Ursule
Molinaro (New York: Bantam, 1971), pp. 17, 15, 277, 26.

    9. Ibid., p. 60.

    10. Aldous Huxley, *Brave New World* (New York: Harper &
Row, 1969), p. 53.

    11. Ibid., p. 56.

    12. Ibid.

    13. Ibid., p. 57.

14. For modern reappraisals of the Pharisees, consult, for example, J. Bowker, *Jesus and the Pharisees* (Cambridge: Cambridge University Press, 1973; Richard A. Burridge, *Four Gospels, One Jesus?* (London: SPCK, 1994); and Jacob Neusner, *From Politics to Piety* (Englewood Cliffs, NJ: Prentice-Hall, 1973).

15. John Stuart Mill, *Utilitarianism* (New York: E. P. Dutton, 1951), p. 16 (chapter 2).

16. J. F. Powers, *Morte d'Urban* (Garden City, NY: Image, 1967), p. 28.

17. Ibid., p. 14.

18. Ibid., p. 25.

19. Ibid., p. 21.

20. Pierre Teilhard de Chardin, *The Divine Milieu* (New York: Harper & Row, 1960), p. 18.

21. Karol Wojtyla, "Girl disappointed in love," in *Easter Vigil and Other Poems,* trans. Jerzy Peterkiewicz (New York: Random House, 1979), p. 42.

Chapter Three.

The chapter epigraph is from Robinson Jeffers, "The Soul's Desert," in *Selected Poems* (New York: Vintage, 1965).

1. Pierre Teilhard de Chardin, *The Divine Milieu* (New York: Harper & Row, 1960), p. 18.

2. Thomas Merton, *New Seeds of Contemplation* (New York: New Directions, 1961), p. 5.

3. Karl Rahner, *Faith in a Wintry Season,* eds. Paul Imhof, Hubert Biallowons, Harvey D. Egan (New York: Crossroad, 1991), p. 91.

4. Alfred North Whitehead, *Process and Reality,* Corrected Edition, eds. David Ray Griffin, Donald W. Sherburne (New York: Free Press, 1978). Whitehead is a notoriously (and needlessly!) difficult author. For a less dense discussion of the fallacy of misplaced concreteness, see his *Science and the Modern World* (New York: Free Press, 1953), pp. 51–60.

5. Julian of Norwich, *Revelation of Love,* trans. John Skinner (New York: Image, 1996), p. 65 [chapter 33].

6. Thomas Merton, *The Seven Storey Mountain* (New York: Harcourt Brace Jovanovich, 1976), p. 205. Merton makes the same point in his poem "Two Desert Fathers," in *Collected Poems* (New York: New Directions, 1977), p. 169:

...our minds, lovers of map and line
Charting the way to heaven with a peck of compasses,
Plotting to catch our Christ between some numbered parallels,
Trick us with too much logic...

7. Francis Dojun Cook tells the story of Hsiang-yen in *How to Raise an Ox* (Los Angeles: Center Publications, 1993), p. 104.

8. See, for example, Chapters 12–15 of Teresa's *Autobiography,* trans. E. Allison Peers (New York: Doubleday, 1991), pp. 134–62, and the Prologue to John's *The Ascent of Mount Carmel,* in *Collected Works,* trans. Kieran Kavanaugh, O.C.D. and Otilio Rodriguez, O.C.D. (Washington, D.C.: ICS Publications, 1991), pp. 115–17.

9. Kierkegaard's discussion of the aesthete is found in Volume 1 of *Either/Or,* trans. David F. Swenson and Lillian Marvin Swenson (Princeton: Princeton University Press, 1971).

10. Aldous Huxley, *Brave New World* (New York: Harper & Row, 1969), p. 57.

11. Thomas Merton, *New Seeds of Contemplation,* p. 187.

12. Abraham Heschel, *A Passion for Truth* (Woodstock, VT: Jewish Lights, 1995), pp. 58–59.

Notes

13. D. H. Lawrence, *Studies in Classic American Literature* (London: Martin Secker, 1933), p. 16.

14. Søren Kierkegaard, *Stages on Life's Way*, trans. Walter Lowrie (Princeton: Princeton University Press, 1940), p. 343.

15. Johannes Tauler, *Second Sermon for the 20th Sunday after Trinity.* Quoted in Reginald Garrigou-LaGrange, *Christian Perfection and Contemplation* (London: Herder & Herder, 1937), p. 393.

16. Thomas Merton, *New Seeds of Contemplation*, p. 83.

17. Mircea Eliade, *Patterns in Comparative Religion*, trans. Rosemary Sheed (New York: Meridian, 1963), p. 30.

18. Jack Clemo, "Growing in Grace," in *The New Oxford Book of Christian Verse*, ed. Donald Davie (New York: Oxford University Press, 1988), p. 290.

19. John Calvin, *Commentary on Psalm 30:6; Sermon Number 8 on I Corinthians.* Quoted in William J. Bouwsma, *John Calvin: A Sixteenth Century Portrait* (New York: Oxford University Press, 1988), p. 47.

20. Rainer Maria Rilke, "Duino Elegy 1," in *Selected Poetry*, trans. Stephen Mitchell (New York: Vintage, 1989), p. 151.

21. Karl Rahner, "The Experience of God Today," in *Theological Investigations XI*, trans. David Bourke (New York: Seabury Press, 1974), p. 159.

22. Ibid.

23. Karl Rahner, "The Logic of Concrete Individual Knowledge in Ignatius Loyola," in *The Dynamic Element in the Church*, trans. W. J. O'Hara (New York: Herder & Herder, 1964), pp. 96–97.

24. Karl Rahner, "Experiencing the Spirit," in *The Practice of Faith: A Handbook of Contemporary Spirituality*, eds. Karl Lehmann, Albert Raffelt (New York: Crossroad, 1983), p. 81.

25. Søren Kierkegaard, *Attack upon Christendom,* trans. Walter Lowrie (Boston: Beacon Press, 1944), p. 82.

26. Ibid., p. 91.

27. Ibid., p. 219.

28. Ibid., p. 221.

29. Ibid.

30. John Calvin, *Sermon Number 48 on Job.* Quoted in Bouwsma, p. 46.

31. Peter Bowles, *The Sheltering Sky* (Hopewell, NJ: Ecco Press, 1977), p. 101.

32. Thomas Merton, *New Seeds of Contemplation,* p. 235.

33. John of the Cross, "Stanzas of the soul that suffers with longing to see God," in *Collected Works,* p. 55.

Chapter Four.

The chapter epigraph is from Robert Lowell, "After the Surprising Conversion," in *Lord Weary's Castle and The Mills of the Kavanaughs* (New York: Harcourt, Brace & World, 1951).

1. R. S. Thomas, "This to Do," in *Pietà* (London: Rupert Hart-Davis, 1966), p. 12.

2. Karl Rahner, "The Divided and Enigmatic Nature of Humanity," in *The Content of Faith: The Best of Karl Rahner's Theological Writings,* eds. Karl Lehmann, Albert Raffelt, and Harvey D. Egan (New York: Crossroad, 1992), p. 120.

Notes

3. Meister Eckhart, *Sermon 1,* in *Meister Eckhart: A Modern Translation,* trans. Raymond Bernard Blakney (New York: Harper & Row, 1941), p. 97.

4. Ibid., p. 102.

5. Ibid., p. 102; see also *Sermon 2,* p. 105.

6. Thomas Merton, *New Seeds of Contemplation* (New York: New Directions, 1961), pp. 34, 35.

7. Thomas Merton, *No Man is an Island* (New York: Harcourt Brace, 1983), p. 125.

8. Rupert Brooke, "The Night Journey," in *Works* (Hertfordshire: Wordsworth, 1994), p. 113.

9. John Berryman, "Great flaming God, bend to my troubles, dear," in *Henry's Fate & Other Poems, 1967–1972* (New York: Farrar, Straus and Giroux, 1977), p. 45.

10. Abraham Heschel, *A Passion for Truth* (Woodstock, VT: Jewish Lights, 1995), pp. 228–29.

11. Albert Camus, *Caligula* (Paris: Gallimard, 1947), pp. 130–31.

12. John of the Cross, *The Dark Night* in *Collected Works,* trans. Kieran Kavanaugh, O.C.D. and Otilio Rodriguez, O.C.D. (Washington, D.C.: ICS Publications, 1991), Book 1, pp. 360–94.

13. Wallace Stevens's comments are in a letter from John Berryman, who wrote to ask for clarification of Stevens's poem "On an Old Horn." Stevens's reply is hardly less cryptic than the poem itself. Quoted in Paul Mariani, *Dream Song: A Life of John Berryman* (New York: Paragon House, 1992), p. 105.

14. Frankl discusses his death-camp experiences in many books, but the single best treatment remains *Man's Search for Meaning: An Introduction to Logotherapy* (Boston: Beacon, 1959).

15. John of the Cross, *The Dark Night* in *Collected Works,* Book 2, pp. 395–457.

16. Simone Weil, *Gravity and Grace,* trans. Arthur Wills (New York: G. P. Putnam, 1952), p. 78.

17. Denise Levertov, "A Heresy," in *The Stream and the Sapphire* (New York: New Directions, 1997), p. 69.

18. Simone Weil, *Gravity and Grace,* p. 84.

19. Catherine of Genoa, *Purgation and Purgatory,* trans. Serge Hughes (New York: Paulist Press, 1979), pp. 85, 86.

20. Simone Weil, *Gravity and Grace,* p. 79.

21. Gershom Scholem, *Major Trends in Jewish Mysticism* (New York: Schocken, 1995), p. 261.

22. Simone Weil, *Gravity and Grace,* p. 108.

23. Catherine of Genoa, *Purgation and Purgatory,* p. 86.

24. Catherine of Genoa, *The Spiritual Dialogue,* trans. Serge Hughes (New York: Paulist Press, 1979), p. 131.

25. Michael Ondaatje chants the many names of the desert in his beautiful and heartbreaking novel *The English Patient* (New York: Random House, 1992), pp. 16–17.

26. Jim Crace, *Quarantine* (New York: Farrar, Straus & Giroux, 1998), p. 192.

27. Ibid., p. 191.

28. Ibid., p. 193.

Chapter Five.

The chapter epigraph is from Jessica Powers, "Pure Desert," in *Selected Poetry of Jessica Powers,* eds. Regina Siegfried and Robert Morneau (Kansas City, MO: Sheed & Ward, 1989).

Notes

1. Martin Buber, *Tales of the Hasidim* (New York: Schocken, 1991), Vol. 1, p. 104.

2. Anonymous, *The Cloud of Unknowing,* ed. William Johnston (New York: Doubleday, 1973), p. 107 [chapter 46].

3. Hart Crane, "Forgetfulness," in *The Complete Poems and Selected Letters,* ed. Brom Weber (Garden City, NY: Doubleday, 1966), p. 137.

4. William Shakespeare, *Timon,* in *Complete Works* (New York: Oxford University Press, 1938), Act V, Scene 1.

5. Meister Eckhart, *Breakthrough: Meister Eckhart's Creation Spirituality in New Translation,* trans. Matthew Fox (Garden City, NY: Doubleday, 1980), p. 183; see also *Sermon 2,* in *Meister Eckhart: A Modern Translation,* trans. Raymond B. Blakney (New York: Harper & Row, 1941), p. 104.

6. Julian of Norwich, *Revelation of Love,* trans. John Skinner (New York: Doubleday, 1997), p. 26 [Chapter 11].

7. Meister Eckhart, *Sermon 4,* in Blakney, p. 119.

8. Ibid., *Sermon 5,* in Blakney, p. 126.

9. Martin Buber, *I and Thou* (2nd edition), trans. Ronald Gregor Smith (New York: Charles Scribner's Sons, 1958), p. 11.

10. Ibid., pp. 11–12.

11. Thomas Merton, *The Asian Journal,* eds. Naomi Burton, Patrick Hart, and James Laughlin (New York: New Directions, 1975), p. 308.

12. *"Nada, nada, nada"* comes from John's sketch of Mount Carmel or the "Mount of Perfection" (he called it both) that illustrates his idea of the soul's journey to God. The route to the mountain's summit is labeled *nada;* as the soul ascends, it becomes *nada;* and when it reaches the top, it finds there *nada.* John's drawing is

reproduced in *The Collected Works of St. John of the Cross,* trans. Kieran Kavanaugh, O.C.D. and Otilio Rogriquez, O.C.D. (Washington, D.C.: ICS Publications, 1991), pp. 110–11.

13. In my discussion of *Khora,* and particularly its development by postmodern thinkers such as Jacques Derrida, I'm indebted to several rewarding conversations with Professor Ilse Bulhof, University of Ultrecht, Netherlands.

14. Plato, *Timaeus,* trans. Benjamin Jowett, in *Collected Dialogues,* eds. Edith Hamilton and Huntington Cairns (Princeton: Princeton University Press, 1973), 49a.

15. Ibid.

16. Ibid., 51a–c.

17. Although Plato comes close to making the identity in 53b.

18. *Chandogya Upanishad,* in *The Upanishads: Breath of the Eternal,* trans. Swami Prabhavananda and Frederick Manchester (New York: New American Library, 1957), p. 70.

19. John Ruusbroec, *The Spiritual Espousals and Other Works,* ed. James A. Wiseman (New York: Paulist Press, 1985), p. 133.

20. Maximus the Confessor, *Selected Works,* ed. George C. Berthold (New York: Paulist Press, 1985), p. 186.

21. Augustine, *Sermo 52,* in *Patrologiae Cursus Completus: Series Latina,* ed. Jacques Paul Migne (Paris: Migne, 1844–1890), Vol. 38, p. 360.

22. Gregory of Nyssa, *Contra Eunomium,* in *Patrologiae Cursus Completus: Series Graeca,* ed. Jacques Paul Migne (Paris: Migne, 1857–1866), Vol. 45, p. 1108.

23. Jacques Derrida, *"Khora,"* in *On the Name,* trans. David Wood, John P. Leavey, Jr., and Ian McLeod (Stanford, CA: Stanford University Press, 1995), pp. 89–127. Pertinent also is Derrida's

Notes

"How to Avoid Speaking: Denials," in *Derrida and Negative Theology*, eds. Harold Coward and Toby Foshay (Albany, NY: State University of New York Press, 1992).

24. Meister Eckhart, *Deutsche Predigten und Traktate*, ed. J. Quint (München: C. Hanser, 1977), pp. 229–30.

25. Meister Eckhart, *Fragments*, in Blakney, p. 233.

26. T. S. Eliot, "Burnt Norton," in *The Complete Poems and Plays, 1909–1950* (New York: Harcourt, Brace & World, 1970), p. 121.

27. For illuminating discussions of the parable's indirect mode of communication, see John Dominic Crossan, *The Dark Interval: Towards a Theology of Story* (Niles, IL: Argus, 1975) and Pheme Perkins, *Hearing the Parables of Jesus* (New York: Paulist Press, 1981).

28. Meister Eckhart, *Sermon 3*, in Blakney, p. 115.

29. Ibid., *Sermon 1*, pp. 96, 97.

30. Ibid., *Sermon 3*, p. 115.

31. Ibid., *Sermon 4*, p. 118.

32. Ibid., *Sermon 5*, p. 126. Dame Julian makes a similar point when she speaks about the necessity to become "nawt" as God is "nawt." See her *Revelation of Love*, especially chapter 18.

33. Meister Eckhart, *Sermon 5* and *Sermon 3*, in Blakney, pp. 127, 117.

34. Ibid., *Sermon 28* and *Sermon 18*, pp. 232, 181.

35. Gerard Manley Hopkins, "That Nature is a Heraclitean Fire and of the Comfort of the Resurrection," in *Poems and Prose*, ed. W. H. Gardner (New York: Penguin, 1984), p. 66.

36. Meister Eckhart, *Sermon 28*, in Blakney, p. 232.

37. Ibid., *Sermon 2*, p. 103.

38. *Chandogya Upanishad*, in Prabhavananda and Manchester, p. 70.

39. Simone Weil, "Forms of the Implicit Love of God," in *Waiting for God*, trans. Emma Craufurd (New York: Harper & Row, 1951), especially pp. 144–49.

40. Meister Eckhart, *Sermon 28*, in Blakney, p. 231.

41. Ibid., *Sermon 7*, p. 134.

42. Ibid., *Sermon 6*, p. 128.

43. It's as much scandal as tragedy that the poetry of Jessica Powers (1905–1988) hasn't yet received the recognition it so deserves. She's one of the finest mystical poets of the twentieth century. It doesn't help that her volumes were all either privately or obscurely printed, and so incredibly hard to locate. Readers who wish to explore her world can track down the recent but already out-of-print *Selected Poetry of Jessica Powers,* eds. Regina Siegfried and Robert Morneau (Kansas City, MO: Sheed & Ward, 1989), Marcianne Kappes's still available *Track of the Mystic: The Spirituality of Jessica Powers* (Kansas City, MO: Sheed & Ward, 1994), which quotes generously from Powers's poetry, or the upcoming *Poetry as Prayer: Jessica Powers* by Robert F. Morneau and Joseph Karlik (Boston, MA: Pauline Books and Media, publication projected for late 2000).

44. Carlo Carretto, *In Search of the Beyond* (London: Darton Longman & Todd, 1975), p. 17.

45. Meister Eckhart, *Sermon 1*, in Blakney, p. 99.

46. Evagrios Ponticus, *The Praktikos: Chapters on Prayer,* ed. John Eudes Bamberger (Spencer, MA: Cistercian Publications, 1970), p. 14.

Chapter Six.

The chapter epigraph is from Sylvia Plath, "The Hanging Man," in *Ariel* (New York: HarperCollins, 1999).

1. Thomas Merton, *New Seeds of Contemplation* (New York: New Directions, 1961), p. 80.

2. Meister Eckhart, *Sermon 3,* in *Meister Eckhart: A New Translation,* trans. Raymond B. Blakney (New York: Harper, 1941), p. 111.

3. D. T. Suzuki, *Outlines of Mahayana Buddhism* (New York: Schocken, 1970), pp. 292–93.

4. Meister Eckhart, *Sermon 3,* in Blakney, p. 111.

5. Abraham J. Heschel, *The Prophets* (New York: Harper & Row, 1962), Vol. 2, p. 1.

6. Matthew Fox, *The Coming of the Cosmic Christ* (San Francisco: Harper & Row, 1988), p. 63.

7. Julian of Norwich, *Revelation of Love,* trans. John Skinner (New York: Doubleday, 1996), p. 181 [chapter 86].

8. Abraham Heschel, *The Prophets,* Vol. 2, p. 3.

9. Abraham Heschel, *A Passion for Truth* (Woodstock, VT: Jewish Lights, 1995), p. 67.

10. Ibid., p. 66.

11. Jung writes about shadow projection in many places, but see especially his *Two Essays on Analytical Psychology,* trans. R.F.C. Hull (New York: Meridian, 1956).

12. Here's what Lewis says in his essay "The Weight of Glory": "There are no *ordinary* people. You have never talked to a mere mortal. Nations, cultures, arts, civilisations—these are mortal, and

their life is to ours as the life of a gnat. But it is immortals whom we joke with, work with, marry, snub, and exploit....Next to the Blessed Sacrament itself, your neighbour is the holiest object presented to your senses." In *The Weight of Glory and other Addresses,* ed. Walter Hooper (New York: Collier, 1980), p. 19.

13. Denise Levertov, "Embracing the Multipede," in *Evening Train* (New York: New Directions, 1992), p. 107.

14. Meister Eckhart, *Breakthrough: Meister Eckhart's Creation Spirituality in New Translation,* trans. Matthew Fox (Garden City, NY: Doubleday, 1980), p. 44.

15. Thomas Merton, *Thoughts in Solitude* (New York: Farrar, Straus, Giroux, 1958), p. 16.

16. Johann Metz, *Poverty of Spirit,* trans. John Drury (New York: Paulist Press, 1968), p. 45.

17. Kathleen Norris wisely discusses the importance of doing God's work in the "everyday" in *The Quotidian Mysteries: Laundry, Liturgy, and "Women's Work"* (New York: Paulist Press, 1998).

18. John Keble, "Morning Hymn," in *The New Oxford Book of Christian Verse,* ed. Donald Davie (New York: Oxford University Press, 1988), p. 217.

19. Karl Rahner, "Prayer in the Everyday," in *The Need and the Blessing of Prayer,* trans. Bruce Gillette (Collegeville, MN: Liturgical Press, 1997), pp. 46, 47.

20. Thomas Merton, "St. John Baptist," in *Collected Poems* (New York: New Directions, 1977), pp. 123–24.

21. Walter Brueggemann, *Hopeful Imagination: Prophetic Voices in Exile* (Philadelphia: Fortress Press, 1986), Chapter 1.

22. Kathleen Norris, *Amazing Grace: A Vocabulary of Faith* (New York: Riverhead Books, 1998), p. 330.

23. Ibid.

24. Ibid., p. 332.

25. Ibid., p. 331.

26. Ibid., p. 332.

27. Karl Rahner, "Laughter," in *The Content of Faith: The Best of Karl Rahner's Theological Writings,* eds. Karl Lehmann, Albert Raffelt, and Harvey D. Egan (New York: Crossroad, 1992), p. 150.

28. Ibid.

29. Ibid., p. 152.

30. Plato, *Ion,* trans. Lane Cooper, in *Collected Dialogues,* eds. Edith Hamilton and Huntington Cairns (Princeton: Princeton University Press, 1973), 533d–34e.

31. Thomas Merton, "Advice to a Young Prophet," in *Collected Poems,* p. 339.

Publisher's acknowledgments from page viii continued—
Excerpt from *The Selected Poetry of Jessica Powers* published by ICS Publications, Washington, D.C. All copyrights, Carmelite Monastery, Pewaukee, WI. Used with permission. Excerpt from *The Collected Works of St. John of the Cross* translated by Kieran Kavanaugh and Otilio Rodriguez. Copyright 1979, 1991 by Washington Province of Discalced Carmelites. Published by ICS Publications, 2131 Lincoln Road, N.E., Washington, D.C. 20002–1199. Used with permission. Excerpt from *The Complete Poems of Hart Crane*, edited by Marc Simon. Copyright 1933, 1958, 1966 by Liveright Publishing Corporation. Copyright 1986 by Marc Simon. Used by permission of W. W. Norton & Co., Inc. Excerpts from "Duino Elegy 1" from *Selected Poetry* by Rainer Maria Rilke. Copyright 1989. Reprinted by permission of Random House, Inc. Excerpt from *The Selected Poetry of Robinson Jeffers* by Robinson Jeffers. Copyright 1941 by Robinson Jeffers. Reprinted by permission of Random House, Inc. Excerpt from *Evening Train* by Denise Levertov. Copyright 1992 by Denise Levertov. Reprinted by permission of New Directions Publishing Corp. and Laurence Pollinger, Ltd. Excerpt from *The Stream and the Sapphire* by Denise Levertov. Copyright 1977 by Denise Levertov. Reprinted by permission of New Directions Publishing Corp. and Laurence Pollinger, Ltd. Excerpts from *The Collected Poems of Thomas Merton* by Thomas Merton. Copyright 1963 by The Abbey of Gethsemani, Inc., 1977 by The Trustees of the Merton Legacy Trust. Reprinted by permission of New Directions Publishing Corp. and Laurence Pollinger, Ltd. Excerpt from "After the Surprising Conversion" in *Lord Weary's Castle* by Robert Lowell. Copyright 1946 and renewed in 1974 by Robert Lowell. Reprinted by permission of Harcourt, Inc., and Faber and Faber, Ltd. Excerpt from *The Poetry of Robert Frost*, edited by Edward Connery Lathem. Copyright 1936 by Robert Frost. Copyright 1964 by Lesley Frost Ballantine. Copyright 1969 by Henry Holt and Co. Reprinted by permission of Henry Holt and Company, LLC. Excerpt from *House of Light* by Mary Oliver. Copyright 1990 by Mary Oliver. Reprinted by permission of Beacon Press, Boston.

Other books by Kerry Walters,
published by Paulist Press——

Godlust: Facing the Demonic,
                    Embracing the Divine

Spirituality of the Handmaid